AMERICA MADE ME A BLACK MAN

AMERICA MADE ME A BLACK MAN

A MEMOIR

BOYAH J. FARAH

SCRIBNER

LONDON NEW YORK SYDNEY TORONTO NEW DELHI

First published in the United States by Harper,
an imprint of HarperCollins Publishers, 2022

First published in Great Britain by Scribner,
an imprint of Simon & Schuster UK Ltd, 2022

1 3 5 7 9 10 8 6 4 2

Simon & Schuster UK Ltd
1st Floor
222 Gray's Inn Road
London WC1X 8HB

www.simonandschuster.co.uk
www.simonandschuster.com.au
www.simonandschuster.co.in

Simon & Schuster Australia, Sydney
Simon & Schuster India, New Delhi

The author and publishers have made all reasonable efforts to contact
copyright-holders for permission, and apologise for any omissions or errors in the form
of credits given. Corrections may be made to future printings.

A CIP catalogue record for this book
is available from the British Library

Hardback ISBN: 978-1-3985-0482-0
eBook ISBN: 978-1-3985-0483-7

Designed by Leah Carlson-Stanisic
Printed in the UK by CPI Group (UK) Ltd, Croydon, CR0 4YY

AS LONG AS YOU THINK YOU'RE WHITE, I'M GOING TO BE FORCED TO THINK I'M BLACK.

—JAMES BALDWIN

AUTHOR'S NOTE

I HAVE CHANGED SOME NAMES, IDENTIFYING FEATURES, AND circumstances in this book, including physical descriptions, occupations, and locations, to preserve the anonymity of the people involved. I have created composite characters and compressed timelines to maintain narrative flow. And while conversations come from my keen recollection, I have not written them to represent word-for-word documentation; rather, I've recounted them in a way that is true to the real feeling and meaning of what was said. In all cases, I have upheld the integrity and essential truthfulness of my story.

AMERICA MADE ME A BLACK MAN

IT'S A COLD, SNOWY EVENING IN BOSTON. SLEEP DOES NOT come to bless me with relief.

A restless insomnia burns inside me from watching George Floyd get lynched by four Minnesota police officers. His dying words haunt me. I am George.

I have black skin.

As night turns into morning, people—cops, former coworkers, all those who call themselves white—surround me, prowl around inside me. Daily demons afflict me from within. I can't untangle myself. Night after night, my eyes refuse to listen. They won't close long enough to allow me a minute's rest. My suffering obeys its own law.

There's no break for my mind. It gallops forward, relentlessly.

My eyes.

My eyes mutiny against me because I'm on the run. I have to keep running from these racist ghouls. Something keeps dragging me backward, tightening its grip on my heart in the middle of the night. In daylight, I can name them. I know who they are and often find myself forced to interact with them. I am tired.

My body hurts. My legs. My back.

Now, this morning, it's my neck. My stomach. Everything hurts.

I am even losing my hair. I am alive, but barely.

This was not my plan thirty years ago when I arrived with my family in America as a war refugee. To die is one thing, but to be torn apart and dismembered by constant fear is something else. The day is just falling into night again, and street-lights are beginning to illuminate the road. Driving on the highway seems to ease the hurt inside.

Driving and listening to music is my medicine, as calming as any therapy.

As I drive, I am watching everything—the cars, trucks, coffee shops, buildings, anyone walking or sitting, hanging out.

I steer along narrow back roads. Then I get onto the freeway, a road to nowhere.

A road to anywhere. A road to everywhere.

I have no particular aim. I just want freedom. To feel the wheels under me rolling. It has been some months since George Floyd was executed. Driving while black at this moment is not a neutral act. I'm fully aware I'm in genuine danger. I feel trapped in the maze of my obsessive thoughts. So I get off the highway and cruise slowly through small-town America, through a vast white universe full of empty streets. In my rearview mirror, I notice a police vehicle and, without really thinking, I reach down to adjust my seat belt.

I want to make sure it is fastened.

I know instinctively that I am about to be pulled over. I steel myself.

Every cell of my body is getting ready. Sure enough, the cop car follows me to a traffic light. As the light turns green,

I don't have time to press down on the accelerator before he hits his siren. It wails insanely loud. As calmly as I can, I signal that I am pulling over to the side. Then I come to a complete stop.

A white policeman steps out. He ambles up to the driver's side of my car. Standing aggressively, he bores the pinpoints of his eyes into me with a penetrating, pitiless gaze. "License and registration," he demands.

His words carry the weight of my body in his hands.

I am alone. I feel alone in America because I know the mortal danger.

"Sorry, Officer," I say, complying totally, trying not to give him an excuse to escalate. I reach for my wallet. His hand sits on his pistol. His eyes seem to laser through my being, alert to any so-called dangerous move on my part. "I'm so sorry."

My eyes, in turn, focus on him, conscious of his every move, as he is conscious of mine. He stands there motionless. Finally I offer him my driver's license.

"I'm just driving through, Officer. I have to find the registration."

I know that he has no reason to stop me, but my experience in America has humbled me. He can take my life in an instant, so I give him what he asks for, forcing myself to smile through my terror. He takes my license and stalks back to his vehicle.

My nervous eyes continue to follow him. I couldn't care less about getting a ticket.

As long as I am unhurt.

Looking around me, I see a white couple jogging under the streetlights. Nothing else disturbs the crystal silence of the night. I am desperately frightened. My lips begin to twitch uncontrollably, an involuntary shivering. Quickly, I put my hand up and rub my mouth.

After a few moments, he slowly returns, each step a deliberate move, anticipating trouble to erupt. He has readied himself to defend his white body against my black body.

"Here you go," he says, handing me my license, along with the ticket he just issued.

Accepting it gratefully, I examine the amount. It is expensive. Two hundred dollars. Maybe I deserve this ticket for driving too slow.

"Hmm," I murmur to myself.

My mind wants to argue. But my nervously quivering lips refuse to allow me to respond properly. He continues to study me, holding himself in a battle-ready stance to react to any false move I might make. He's completely unaware of the quarrel he has provoked within my spirit. It is hard to digest this injustice.

"You were speeding," he lies.

"No way, Officer," I say, surprising myself. "I wasn't speeding at all."

"Tell it to the judge." He smiles.

The tone of his lying words, the pitiless glare of his white gaze. Right now, this man's eyes vibrate with whiteness—with confidence in his supremacy. The entitled posture of his body and the delicate but threatening way his fingers linger over his pistol instantly convey to me his intention, his manufactured and unapologetic justification for pulling me over when I have done absolutely nothing wrong.

"Okay, Officer," I say, cooperating. "Thanks. Have a good night, sir."

None of these words rise from an honest place in me.

Fear of having my body injured dominates my mental calculus, fear of what George Floyd was forced to experience as his life was suffocated out of him.

His sad crying out for his dead mother, his excruciating pleas for air, his haunting repeated "I can't breathe," his awareness of imminent death, his submission beneath the brutal white knee of that white psychopath.

None of that is alien to black bodies living in America.

I can feel George Floyd's words as if I am speaking them myself.

It could have been me. I could have been George Floyd that day.

"If you have a problem with it, take it up in court" are the officer's last words as he struts back to his cruiser. I watch him snatch at the door, yank it open, and slip smoothly inside, like a snake.

I remain still. I place my hand on my forehead.

The sweat is dripping down my nose, the sides of my face, my chin.

It is cold, yet my body is soaked with perspiration, as if I've been running for miles. I have been running, just not in the normal way with my legs and feet.

Alone, I talk to myself. "How can my safety be left in the hands of a white cop?"

I wait patiently for him to pull away. Only then do I hit the engine and roll out. I turn around, returning to the city.

Just going for a simple drive almost killed me.

2

GEORGE W. BUSH WAS ELECTED AND 9/11 HAPPENED WHILE I
was in college, part of the educated class in America, a National Public Radio listener, and a reader of the *New York Times*.
My world was beginning to take shape. President Bush was in
full war rhetoric, and the news media was looping scenes of
the soft-spoken Osama bin Laden sitting with a Kalashnikov in
a cave somewhere in the mountains of Afghanistan. President
Bush's words—*Every nation in every region now has a decision to
make. Either you are with us, or you are with the terrorists*—were
taking his country, my adopted country, into the hell of war.

Those drumbeats of war upset my belly. I knew something
about such words of war, and those bloody memories were still
crying inside me. Although I feared war and its path toward
mighty destruction, I was still excited for myself: I was the
first in my family to graduate from university. Whether in the
car or walking and sipping coffee, I continued to absorb hope
from the melody pouring into my ears. Despite the rumor of
war, I thought I could dance with it, tolerate it. I was intox-
icated, and never did it occur to me that my situation might
make a lion break down into tears: to be a man and to cry
can't mix in the same belly, I thought. My African eyes didn't

belong to tears. I knew something about war, but America was on the verge of teaching me that she owned my body. My actions. My emotions. My daily interactions with the outside world. The music pouring into my ears made me think that I was in control of my soul, but in reality, America was in complete control of me. I heard Kanye West declare on live television, "George Bush doesn't care about black people," but I was not listening. I did not understand. I was neither black nor white: in Africa, I was my departed father's son, but in America I was nobody's son.

When I applied for my first job, I was really excited about it. My optimism was at its peak. Despite the warmongering dominating the airways, I felt as if I were just being born, as if the world and everything in it was only just beginning to shine. I was drunk with happiness. I had to learn over time that you can run away from the gathering clouds of war, but you cannot hide or escape: it penetrates your body before you even have time to react. And if you do react, you have nowhere to run, and danger awaits your body everywhere. The atrocity of war is immediate, but the pain inflicted on the body by communal hatred is gradual and piercing and seizes your body quietly, without you noticing it.

At the time I thought: Today, I am no longer a refugee. My life is changed, and I am in the land of the free. Perhaps for the better. I have a job of my own, an apartment of my own, a car with insurance, health care, a primary care doctor of my own, food, clothes, gas money, occasional movie nights and other lifestyle expenses. I consider myself an American with all the American necessities, and I have an American friend at work named Deric. But I am noticing a different kind of danger rising and falling before my eyes, and it is unlike any other danger

I have known. During the day, I can fight off this enormous fear, but there is nothing I can do about it when it interrupts my night and refuses to let me close my eyes.

Deric and I are sitting at lunch again as usual. He orders spaghetti with a can of Coke, and I get a cheeseburger with Sprite. Outside the wide glass of the window, snow is falling, covering the green grass.

"When did you land this job?" Deric asks me.

"Just before I graduated from college in 2002. I remember the exact moment the offer came and how excited I was."

"That was a really crazy time," he says. "Do you remember?"

When I got the call about the job, I was driving along the Charles River. The phone buzzed in my pants pocket like a jackhammer digging a hole on the side of the road, and I knew it was from the job I'd applied to, so I flipped the phone open with a smile.

"Hello," I said.

I'd picked up the habit of watching people's lips as they spoke while I was learning English, so I could try to trace the origin of their accent. But over the phone, picking out different accents was more difficult. The woman on the other side of the phone—whose accent I couldn't place—offered me the job. "You have time to think about it," she said.

"No, I accept the position," I said quickly. I did not want to give her a chance to change her mind. "Thank you very much."

"Expect an offer letter in the mail soon."

When she finished, I pulled my car over, parked behind a flat-looking storage building, and got out. I walked down the pavement, turned right onto the trimmed grass, removed my hat, tossed it in the air, and ran after it. I dropped onto the grass, ripped up a handful, put it in my mouth, and spat it out with a smile. I rolled in the grass and sang quietly to myself, "I got the job!" as I lay flat, staring at the blue sky.

A couple jogging by came to a stop, turned around, and looked me in the eyes.

They sat down on the grass too, not far from me, but I didn't mind.

I felt the moisture of joy in my eyes, and the smooth fresh air seeped under my armpits, cooling my body. That job meant everything to me. I could get an apartment. I could support my family. I could send money to my living grandmother, who seemed as old as the earth beneath her feet. I could support a charity to help others living in despair, as I had in those refugee camps. Doing something with passion was all I cared about. I couldn't wait to bring my passion and intellect to this new job, my creativity and diligence. I am a child of two nations. I am an African. I am an American. I want both continents to be proud of me. So many people had been there for me, I thought; now it was my time to be there for them. At that defining moment, the world belonged to this African child of war, now a naturalized American citizen.

The drifting cool air tickled below my ears, and the trees heard my whispered promises. The couple sitting near me on the grass craned their necks in bewilderment, but my thoughts were as honest as the blue sky. Since arriving in New England, I had learned to appreciate the simple things in life: opening my eyes for the first time every morning, noticing the smell of morning breath, feeling hot and cold water in the shower, sipping a cup of English tea, chewing a morsel of oatmeal with slices of banana, walking on the paved roads, seeing the sun, breathing in the clean air, hearing vehicle engines turning on, listening to the singing birds, and hearing the chatter of children walking to school.

Within a few months of landing the job, I began to use my life to motivate others by giving talks. I found great meaning in telling my story: a story of destiny in the making, of war and of refugees, of sickness and death, a love story for America. There was joy too in receiving from listeners such a positive reaction to my story.

I could not sing. I could not rap. I could not play with words in English the way I could in Somali. I could not play ball. I could not run. I could not play the guitar or piano. I could not dance. But in lecturing about my life, it seemed to me that I could work through and reshape my experiences back in Africa, where I had witnessed people weeping over the deaths of their own. Now what I had gone through was not only bringing people to tears but leading them to recite blessings for me. I felt like a different man, as tall as the heavens above the clouds.

3

BACK IN THE COMPANY LUNCHROOM, SITTING ACROSS FROM
my friend Deric, I'm reminiscing. "Believe it or not," I say, "I
was so happy when you got a job here and came on board."

"I was happy too," Deric says. "But I would never have
lasted this long if you had not been here working with me."

"Oh." I stretch the word a bit longer in my lips. "I could say
the same about you too."

During my first several years on the job, I was all alone, the
only black man on staff in my office. And I did often feel lonely.
The experience of America belonged to me, but I did not wish
to become her victim. My earlier experiences in Africa did not
count here, and it seemed I had no say in shaping who I would
become. I was living in the belly of America; it was she who
made me a black man, relegated me to her black tribe. All the
whites on the job stuck together. They often stood around and
talked to one another. They went out and ate lunch together.
They never invited me, but their actions were shaping me,
creating this feeling of loneliness. I ate alone. I sat alone. The
thoughts inside me were alone, and my lips remained careful,
controlled in what I said.

Then Deric joined the team in another department, adjacent

to mine. His first day on the job, I visited him in his new office, just across the hall from mine, and brought two cups of coffee. I had met Deric during my last year of high school, but we did not start hanging out together until college. Although Deric took night classes back then, we used to share the same table in the quiet-study area of the college library, chatting and drinking coffee and joking around on breaks.

Now, years later, we were brothers in arms, close comrades.

His first day on the job, I found a seat in front of Deric's nice desk, and he said, "Let's see how long these white folks are going to leave me alone and let me keep this job." He was joking, wincingly, suggesting real pain under the facetious facade.

"Come on," I said, finding his cynical posture tiresome. "Stop kidding around."

His meaning had escaped me. The fact was, Deric was born here. He carried a cultural memory in his black body that I lacked.

"Well," he said, grinning as if to say I'd have to learn my lesson. "Time will tell, Boyah. Let's just put it like that."

I was pleased when Deric joined, and he was glad I was there too. We collaborated well.

"I tell you," he said. "I'm so happy, man."

He turned on his computer. I calmly took a sip of my hot coffee.

"Me too," I said.

That first day, Deric picked up his framed bachelor's degree from underneath his desk and hung it up on the wall above his computer. "Let's get to work," he said.

"Indeed," I said. Then I changed the conversation. Our nice-nice talk was making me feel soft inside. "This is a great office space. How did you end up with a better one than me?"

Taking another sip of coffee, I waited for his reaction.

"Well"—he chuckled—"look at me." He paused to underline his meaning, spreading his arms out, palms up. "Boyah, isn't it obvious that I'm better-looking?"

"Better-looking? C'mon! Can you see okay?"

Honestly, he wasn't better-looking, but he was striking. Dark-skinned, over three hundred pounds, and six foot five, he was impressive and fit. He was, I had to admit, handsome, and his manner was all about peace and getting along with everyone.

But he did in fact have a large, clean office with two actual windows through which natural sunlight shone.

My tiny cubicle at the back of the main office, on the other hand, was filled with abandoned old papers that belonged to the department and couldn't be removed.

He shrugged, smiling. "I was going to say 'better educated,' but we got the same degree."

"That's right. We graduated together, and now we work here together."

"That's a blessing," he said.

Stepping out of his office, I eased myself through the revolving front door of the building, soaking up all the details of the world around me. The grass, random birds floating beneath the empty blue sky, the construction workers not far away below the highway, wearing yellow hard hats, the billowing smoke over the cement factory, and that snowplow parked in the gray snowdrift off to the side.

Breathing in a cold blast of bright winter air, I headed back to my cubicle.

4

I COME FROM A FARAWAY PLACE. I SPENT MY CHILDHOOD LIV-
ing a nomadic lifestyle in the Nugaal Valley of Somalia with
my grandmother—in Somali, my *ayeyo*. I remember sitting on
a rock, my eyes watching those grazing goats stretching out
across the green valley. Holding a cup filled with foaming camel's milk, I bring it close to my lips and take a sip while I gaze
out over the low trees and red anthill mounds. The Nugaal
Valley, where Egyptian pharaohs are believed to be buried, is
located deep in the Puntland region of Somalia, known as the
Land of Fragrance because the soil actually emanates a per-
fumed scent. Every tree exudes a cologne-like odor that wafts
through the air. Colorful butterflies flutter up and down over
the flowers. I see ants carrying objects on their backs as they
walk like soldiers. I see a fox digging up something from beneath the soil. I see an ostrich with long, muscular legs and
elongated neck, protruding eyes and long lashes, walking and
grazing with her young. I see birds flying low and high before
resting on the low trees in the valley. I see hordes of monkeys
clustered together just over the hill. I see a rainbow forming in
the distance. I see Ayeyo holding a stick and walking through
the grass. There, I am free and without fear.

I have no written record of my birthday. I do not have a birth certificate. I can only approximate what year I was born, but Ayeyo memorized and conveyed to me orally the unbroken history of my family lineage. Her narrative always included the story of my birth and the circumstances surrounding my coming into the world. Although nothing is written down, I know with precision my family genealogy.

Long ago, I was sitting on the soft sand with my *ayeyo*. The sun was warm. A large drop of water fell from the tree branch we were sitting under. It dropped onto a leaf and split into two droplets. I laid my head in her lap. She smelled good, like face powder and lady's perfume and burning incense oil. She was as African as the soil on which we sat.

"What happened when I came out?" I asked her.

Ayeyo turned her gaze from the goats grazing in the valley and told me again the story of my birth. As our eyes met, I wanted to cry.

"You were born because the prayers of many people asking for a son for your father brought you out into the world," she said. Wearing a tailored dress in a yellow, blue, and green pattern, she spoke from a position of wisdom, gained not from the passage of time but from dancing with the angels of death.

When I was born, Ayeyo said, she cupped her hands together and thanked God for answering her prayer. Once the other women heard the commotion, they clapped their hands together and cheered. Their singing tongues rang throughout the hospital. The two nurses ululated, stamped their feet on the ground, and made clicks with their tongues.

A woman was called in to bless me. She burned incense in a mini charcoal burner and lifted it up over Mama and me. She waved it around the room to ward off the evil eye. Drums were beaten while five women stamped their feet and danced around us.

At this part of the story, I usually said, "I always knew that I was a star," grinning widely.

Right after I was born, a sheet of rain began to beat the hospital windows. Wind slapped the leaves. Rain is a rarity in Somalia, falling only three or four times a year. So the occasion of rain was celebrated as a blessing from the Almighty.

"You *are* a star," Ayeyo said, touching my face delicately. "God sent rain for your arrival because you are a blessed child."

As was Somali custom, my father waited in the next room until after the delivery. When he heard the ululations and clapping and singing, joy began to tingle inside him. Happy tears rolled down his cheeks, and he rushed into the room, kissed Mama on the cheek, and looked at me for the first time. Then he took my tiny body, lifted me up in both hands toward the sky in thanksgiving, and handed me back to Mama.

Two hours later Dad drove us home—Mama, Ayeyo, and me, wrapped in a baby sheet.

Dad then went to the Bakaara market and returned with two male goats to be slaughtered, another female goat for milk, and a set of gold earrings with a matching necklace for Mama. Friends brought over cooked rice, meat, and tea. Neighborhood women, men, and children poured into the house. Everyone ate together and drank tea in a festive, euphoric atmosphere.

Ayeyo told me all about it, sitting next to me in the valley beneath that African mountain. My life began as a divine joy.

I was to be the sun shining over my family.

On the seventh day of my life, as the brilliant morning sun broke through, Dad took me from Mama's lap and lifted me up high again. As a thousand tiny rays of blinding sunshine glowed between the houses and the wind swept through my baby hair, my father extended his arms and turned 360 degrees, holding me up toward the furnace of the yellow sun of that morning sky.

A friend of my father who was also enlisted in the army unclipped a magazine from his gun, removed a bullet, and opened it. He dipped his index finger in the gunpowder and placed a dot on my forehead, performing a sacred Somali ritual.

In this way he marked me for life, marked me to be a brave son, a fighter.

"May God protect you, my brave son," Dad whispered proudly. Holding me up against the shining yellow morning horizon, he continued pouring prayers into my ears. "Surely, we belong to God and to him we shall return."

Afterward he grabbed a goat by its legs, slammed it down on the sand, and turned its head facing east. Placing a butcher knife on the goat's neck, he slashed its throat.

Ayeyo hung the goat from a low branch and skinned it.

Spreading a mat on the sand, they placed the liver, stomach, head, and heart on one side and the shoulders, legs, ribs, and neck on the other side. They lit three portable stoves.

On one stove, they placed a pot for the liver, now chopped into small pieces, and added sliced onions, diced tomatoes, green pepper, green chile, cilantro, and coriander. On the other, they made flatbread and cooked rice.

As the aroma of cooking liver wafted through the air, a large kettle of tea hissed on the third portable stove.

One by one, women, men, boys, and girls from the neighborhood came to the house. As they sat in a circle in groups of four, they ate with their right hands and washed the food down with cups of tea. It was understood that when many bellies were fed, those bellies, in turn, would silently whisper prayers for my health and longevity—prayers not only that I'd be welcomed completely into this world but also that I'd get a warm reception in the beyond, when my soul finally drifted into the kingdom of death.

The meat cooking in a large pot on the fire bubbled up and spat as the pot with rice did the same. People sat or stood in the shade. Others leaned their backs against the wall.

Others, mostly men, stood around with their hands in their pants pockets as they puffed on cigarettes. After they ate, a man wearing a traditional handwoven Somali cap and a scarf led the prayers giving me my name. He later became my Quran teacher.

While the men gathered, he murmured prayers in Arabic. Women and children echoed "Amen" simultaneously in low voices.

The imam wore his traditional Somali skullcap pulled forward authoritatively on his head; his beard was reddened with henna, and a red scarf dangled from his neck. He continued murmuring prayers in Arabic. The others raised their voices a bit higher in ululating prayers for me—first in a high pitch, then in a low tone—so that the heavens could hear the glorious names given to me during this ceremony:

Muhammad, after the prophet.

Burhan, which means "gifted."

Abdikafi, "slave of God."

And Libax, "lion."

My life began gloriously. Ayeyo told me all about it. But in the end, I did not like any of my given names, so when I became an American, I gave myself the name Boyah.

Like Dylan, like Malcolm, like Ali, with my new name I am

free. And everything I have, I carry with me. And like the no-mad, I fly and capture the sky in the palm of my hand. I am an American, and this is America, where I am learning to own my identity and claim my new name.

I was so transported that I used to think of myself as not merely a star but the sun.

Raised in the nomadic life deep in the Nugaal Valley, I en-joyed the freedom to be, to roam, to walk, to gaze upward at the drifting sun or the falling moon or the fighting stars in the middle of the night. I had no inkling of the destiny that lay ahead of me.

I come from a faraway place.

5

WHEN I WAS ELEVEN, MY FATHER DIED OF UNTREATED LUNG cancer, and a few months later, civil war broke out and carried us away from Somalia as the wind carries drifting clouds. Now we were refugees—my mother, my older sister, my five younger siblings, and myself—running from violence, running to save our lives from certain death. Our lives seemed destined for despair and destitution.

For almost two years, we ran. Finally we made it to Utanga, a squalid, disease-infested refugee camp located right on the edge of the ancient city of Mombasa in Kenya. Sipping tea and eating white bread day after day, watching the sun rise and waiting for it to set in late afternoon—these were my only memories. Life was dead. Democracy was dead. In Utanga, there was nothing for me except the obligation to lift a shovel and follow the other male refugees as we buried yet another neighbor dead from malaria or dengue fever.

We spent two years in that camp before finally, four years after we were forced into exile by the civil war, we found a sponsor and escaped. I was fifteen when we left the refugee camp. Destiny directed us to Bedford, Massachusetts, a city outside

Boston with a population of thirteen thousand. There, all that was inside me expanded.

I can see myself stepping out of the house and walking to the library, counting the silent houses with dogs peeking out the windows. That certainly is strange, I think. These people live in beautiful houses with big backyards. And the dogs live in the house with them.

This is new to me. I can't figure out why Americans allow dogs to live indoors along with the family. In Somalia, animals stay outside. Inside is only for people. I'm afraid of dogs anyway. And forget about bringing them into the house!

In America, I see no goats, cows, or chickens. Instead, I pass endless front yards with manicured grass and trees swaying slowly in the clean air. All is nestled in a forest of green, a stark contrast with the semidesert landscape of Somalia. No longer in that rotten refugee camp, here I am walking on an American sidewalk with grass on each side, trimmed to perfection.

Since I do not see anyone cut the grass, I imagine that God sends invisible angels to cut the grass at night while the people of Bedford sleep. And God does this because America is a country where democracy lives, and no one is threatened or harmed.

As I walk, I stoop to run my palms over the grass and enjoy how it feels.

I can look at the sky, clear and blue.

I can feel the air.

I can walk on paved roads and grass without sand drifting into my eyes, my food, my hair. I can eat pizza. I can stroll to the supermarket and glance at the different soft drinks, the many types of sausages on display, the endless rows of bright cartons of fresh milk in the store's enormous refrigerator.

Studying the lips of the white people shopping around me, I marvel at the sounds they make, using their strange language. My desire to learn is intense.

I want to talk to them exactly the way they do to each other.

As I walk around the town with my thoughts and dreams, I am conscious of my good fortune in America, ready to undertake what destiny has in store for me.

"Be a doctor," I tell myself aloud. "Yes, you can, Boyah! Or be an engineer!"

My thoughts are my invisible friends, since I have none in this town.

Nor do I see any possibility of these white people becoming friends: nothing about them belongs to me. I do not even meet many people walking. Just an occasional mother pushing her baby in a stroller and sometimes a white couple jogging along the sidewalk.

I am tall and skinny and noticeable in this white suburban town.

I can feel the gaze of the white neighbors, wondering who I am and whether or not I speak their language or eat their food or like their music. I am not one of them, but I am eager to become one of them. As I pass by them, they smile. I keep their smiles as a gesture of goodwill.

They like me, I tell myself hopefully. I wish they could know that I like them too.

Anytime I see someone walking or jogging or sitting on the grass, my lips eagerly form smile after smile. I am thinking that they might be able to grasp the meaning of my many smiles, these strange white people gawking at me with pimpled, freckled faces.

My family and I are the tallest and the blackest in this

all-white town. As I become more aware of this new reality, I sometimes wish I could touch their pale skin and run my fingers through their blond or red hair.

Mama, wearing a long dress with red, blue, and white patterns, walks around the neighborhood sometimes. Because she has no English, she only grins when someone greets her. The white people cannot get to know her as a person, and she cannot express who she is as a fellow human being, so we stand out as those strange refugees who never stop smiling.

Our neighbors never invite us to the neighborhood block party, nor do they stop by for a chat or a brief visit, or spend any length of time with us. But once they figure out that we are not going to cause any trouble and that we are grateful even to be alive in this new land, they begin to interact with us a little.

Someone random, an older white man, says to me one day, "Aren't you from that family on Roberts Drive?"

"Yes," I answer politely. "I'm sorry."

Even though I have not broken any law, I always apologize. I understand his question. Saying sorry is a survival tactic, a way to protect myself.

"How are your folks?" he says. "How many of you live in that house?"

"Uh" is all I say. Then I nod my head. "I'm sorry."

Almost all the houses near us are one-family structures. To the right of us is a house with a husband and wife, two cars, and two dogs. To the left is a big house with a husband and wife, a child, and two dogs. Big backyards with trimmed grass surrounded by metal fences.

In our small house, we are ten people, living on the second floor in a three-bedroom apartment. Along with me and my mother are my three younger brothers and two younger sisters.

My older sister, with the husband she married in the refugee camp, is also there, raising their year-old child. We have to line up and take turns to use the bathroom, but we have no inkling that we are missing anything. We are not yet Americans.

In our small apartment house live different people: white, black, and Asian individuals who come and go. All we know about them is that they are Americans and speak English. Hearing them talk in the hallway, I wish I could learn to speak English like them.

Some representatives of the International Rescue Committee help us by dropping off used clothes, winter jackets and shoes, and a beat-up used bicycle. Everything in the apartment comes from the IRC or from the secondhand shop Mama visits twice a week, sometime three times a week. Our living room is outfitted with a sofa, a love seat, a gray carpet, an old mini television with two tiny speakers, a small coffee table for the tea thermos and three ceramic cups, and an old grandfather clock hanging above the floor lamp. Even our cordless telephone comes from the used-furniture store.

We are the newly arrived, the poor and black living in America.

Sitting in the living room watching *America's Most Wanted* with John Walsh, Mama always draws us around her and reminds us to keep the front door closed. She does not want the constant commotion coming from the first-floor apartment to disturb the calmness in our apartment. Those people on the first floor are Americans, and Mama is aware we are lucky to be here and asks us to respect our host country and respect our American neighbors.

We are happy and appreciative. As I walk to the library, I notice the clear blue sky turning to gray, the air becoming thicker, and the trees beginning to lose their leaves. Slowly, those trees are becoming skeletons, as if they were getting naked for the coming of snow, like couples getting ready to conceive their first child.

The man on the Weather Channel tells me what day and time the snow will fall, but I have trouble believing his prediction. I do not think God communicates directly with human beings, let alone with a white man in a black suit who gets drunk with forbidden liquor and who may not even believe in God. Coming as I am from a place of human catastrophe, my singular worldview has yet to be exposed to the diversity of human beliefs and cultures. Yes, it is late in the afternoon, the daylight is growing shorter, and the sky is becoming grayer, but how does that white man dressed in a suit on television know exactly when the snow will come?

Does the silent sky communicate with him? What kind of relationship can they have?

I want to say something, but I figure no one will understand me.

In my shadowy bedroom, the light is on, and I am reciting to myself a list of English words to memorize. I am on a mission to master the English language and make it my own when suddenly, at precisely the time the weatherman predicted, clumps of snow begin to beat against the glass window of my room. With that, I come to believe in the magic of America.

When I see the snow, my heart seems to skip a beat. I jump up from the couch and quickly run outdoors. Standing on the doorstep, I look up at the gray sky, and my eyes follow the snowflakes pouring down onto the earth and covering everything below in white. The driving snow keeps coming and coming, covering the grass and the sidewalks and the driveway and the paved streets—everything, including the green grass. In front of our neighbor's house next door, children are wearing jackets, gloves, sweaters, and rubber boots as they play in the snow. One has a shovel, another a spoon, and yet another is sitting on a toboggan. As I watch them, I am feeling cold, but something in me is keeping my body warm. I breathe, and mists of fog escape my mouth. I love everything I see. I am overwhelmed. Stretching out my hands and opening my mouth to the sky, I begin to collect snowflakes. I see my younger siblings come running outside and reaching out for the snow, giggling and making all kinds of noises with their tongues. I too attempt to catch the snow falling through the air, but the flakes melt into the palm of my hand, slippery and invisible, but wet. At one time, all of us children are out in the open, and all of us have our mouths tilted up and open in the air to collect the falling snow. My mouth is agape, my teeth chattering. I want to pray to God for a pair of rubber boots and gloves. But then God has already granted my wish to escape war, withstand disease, and survive starvation. How can I be so selfish as to pray for even more? God has already convinced the Americans to let me stand here in the snow and play. Could I ask for more? God is good. The world is good. The falling snow is beautiful, and my belly is full of love, prayers, and hope for my life in America.

I feel a sharp pain in my ears, but I am too busy to pay much attention. I romp through snow, as if coming across a new friend for the first time. I squeeze the snow in the palm of my hand until it hurts. As I collect snow in my mouth, my teeth begin to hurt and my lips crack. My nose is running, and my ears are on fire. I can see that my siblings are having similar snow-triggered symptoms. In the refugee camp, during the resettlement orientation we went to before coming to America, they told us all about snow. They told us how dangerous it could be. They said snow could kill. Still, I always yearned for the experience.

"Get back in here," my mother calls out. "You need something warmer on."

So I rush back into the house and head for the kitchen to turn on the oven. Once the oven heats up, I open the oven door and sit down in front of the heat.

My mother is sitting in front of the television, wrapped in a large blanket, holding a white ceramic cup with hot chocolate. Seeing me shivering in front of the oven, she invites me into the living room. "Come and taste this," she says, holding out her cup to me. "Here, taste it."

"Oh," I say as I take the cup from her hands and sip. "I like that." And then I watch my mother as she begins to get more cups for the kids.

"Keep that for yourself." Mama gets up and walks to the kitchen to make another cup for herself. "But don't go back outside until you put on a heavier jacket, okay?"

I walk up the stairs, enter the room I share with my three brothers, and grab my heavy winter jacket. I put it on and run back downstairs. As my siblings watch me get my jacket, they too get theirs, and we continue playing outside as if nothing in the world existed except our joy in the snow. Once outside again, I am more wary of the cold, the chilly bite in my feet and hands and ears, my runny nose. This time I recognize the danger.

As the danger and beauty of my first year in America passes, spring comes around again. I used to ride my rusty bicycle frequently to visit the library. One afternoon, I slow down at a traffic intersection, but continue through since I have the green light.

Just as I am almost through the intersection, the car that was waiting for the light suddenly takes off and bangs the rear wheel of my bicycle.

I lose control and hit the pavement, landing on my elbows and knees. Quickly getting up and inspecting my injuries, I notice plenty of bloody scratches on my elbows and knees, but I feel embarrassed. I watch as the blue Chevy that hit me parks, and the driver's door opens. An elderly white woman steps out. "I am so sorry," she says sincerely.

"It's okay," I reply, intimidated.

"Let me take you to a doctor," she says.

"No," I insist. "I'm fine."

I am not fine at all, and I am watching blood pour from my elbows and knees. My mangled bicycle is lying in the grass.

"Don't worry about your bicycle," she says nicely. "I'll buy a new bicycle for you."

"No," I say. "It's okay. No need."

"Let me give you some money to fix it," she implores. "I want to take you to a doctor, so you can get some stitches."

"No, it's okay. I'm sorry. Please. Go home."

I feel I owe her. Indeed, I owe her my life.

She is American, and I am not.

I am an African boy whose country is ruined, and this white woman has welcomed me and allowed me into her country. I have come to her house. I walk on her streets.

I am breathing her clean air. I touch and hold her snow.

I walk in her large supermarket. I capture her smiles and hold them dearly. She has done a lot for me, but what have I done for her? Nothing.

Yes, she hit me with her car, and I have scratches that may need some stitches, but that is nothing. I look at my injuries and think that those wounds are nothing compared to the depth of my gratitude for America. She is American; she is free to go.

I pick up my bicycle and start dragging it home.

"Can I take you home?" she asks kindly.

"No. Go home. I'm okay."

As I take those few first steps toward home, I look back and see that woman standing there watching me. My bicycle is old and rusty and fragile, and I am not sure what I am to her. Maybe just a poor young black African in a skinny body.

But this kind old woman is the America of my imagination, new and fascinating.

And dangerous.

6

IT WAS LATE DURING MY SECOND SUMMER IN BEDFORD.

The blue sky was clear. It was close to eighty degrees. Everyone was still wearing shorts, and there were lots of people casually pedaling bikes.

Madeline, my younger brother's grade-school teacher, a woman with a heart wide enough to shelter all humanity, had arranged for me to visit the dentist at one of the fancy university teaching hospitals in Boston.

I went for my appointment, and when the office assistant called out my name, I followed her into the back office. Surrounded by four young dentists wearing white uniforms and holding sharp instruments, I hardly spoke. I found it difficult to initiate conversation with such strange people, their blue eyes, blond hair, bloodless pale pink skin.

I loved the way English words sprang from their mouths and reached out to others almost invisibly. My eyes followed their words until one of the others responded with their own.

Before I got into the dentist's chair, I tried to put them on notice that during the previous visit, they had worked on the wrong tooth and disconnected it from the root. That tooth ached, and I knew something was wrong.

I had a problem with the dentist, but I also had a problem with the language.

In timid, heavily accented English, I stammered words about the past visit, the tooth, the pain. None of them said anything in reply, but I trusted their authority. Once I was settled into that chair and laid out in that submissive position, I suddenly found myself the nameless object of their science.

After taking X-rays, they numbed my mouth and began their work. There I was lying back in their chair, following the conversation. Two dentists were preparing to drill into my mouth, while two other dentists watched.

"Where did you get him from?" the tallest asked.

The fattest dentist appeared confused. "Who?" he said.

"This one," the tall one said, nodding his chin in my direction.

Looking up at him, I caught his smile.

"He's from outside," the fat one replied. "There are plenty of them out there."

There were, indeed, many black homeless people sitting, sleeping, walking, and begging right outside the dental school. I maintained my calm, as if oblivious to the revelations unfolding in their shockingly open and honest conversation, right in front of me to hear.

"Is he getting paid for this?" a short, thin dentist said.

"Not really," the tall dentist said. "This is an odd one, paying with his own insurance."

A disturbing chuckle rose from the short dentist. "You're lucky," he said. "You've got a good quiet one in here who has manners."

"Yeah," the tall dentist said, laughing loudly. "This is a strange one, some kind of third-world refugee kid, or whatever that's supposed to mean. He could be from around the block."

Perhaps they avoided saying my name, thinking I could not pick up what they were talking about. But in fact at the time, their English was beginning to belong to me, slowly.

"Actually, his teeth are pretty good. He's lucky. Coming here must be a luxury for him. He doesn't know how good he's got it here, I bet."

I did not say a word, but their conversation was seeping into my belly.

I felt like shouting to them that of course my teeth are clean and good because I brush my teeth five times a day. In Somalia, it is customary to brush our teeth each time we pray.

Indeed, my ancient African *ayeyo* lived to be over one hundred years old without ever going to a dentist, and with all her unstained teeth intact.

A pool of sweat covered my body.

The thin one chuckled again. "He doesn't speak very much English, does he?"

"No, not at all," the fat one said. "Just a few words."

"Didn't you pay fifty dollars the other day to someone else like him?"

"Yeah," the tall dentist said. "But that one wasn't as patient as this one."

"Maybe we're going to start getting more of these third-world-type refugees like him," the shorter dentist said.

I was a refugee from Somalia at a time when television pictures of starving children with protruding bellies and flies hovering over corpses were all over the news. But I believed that white dentists had to be better human beings than the ones I had left behind in the civil war. And I was just like them.

"Yeah, maybe," the tall dentist said.

"I guess you can do to this one whatever you want," the fat dentist joked.

They laughed uproariously.

What they were doing to me was just a picnic, a mere walk in the park on a rainy day.

"Well, no," the tall dentist said, smirking. "Not really."

"But isn't that what we're doing right now?"

"Well," the tall dentist said. "I'm not really going to argue with you."

My ears were picking up their words, and my eyes were following their demeanor. I started to feel awful. My stomach was beginning to turn. And so, they continued.

"He's a good one," the tall dentist said, finishing up. "We're done."

As I got out of the dentist's chair and walked out into the sunshine, I felt violated. To be lying prostrate in that dentist's chair while they joked about who I was and what I was, it petrified me.

I decided never to go back to the dentist. I never wanted to find myself in that position again. I had barely escaped Somalia's civil war. I had seen other boys my age carry shovels to bury black corpses, dead from disease, and my nostrils still held the inextinguishable memory of that stench, the reek of the half dead or the already dead, littering the refugee camps where I was confined.

There was that man stoned to death, and that young woman with the chiseled face and light dimples who was shot to death—my eyes held witness to those memories. But now all those horrors were behind me, and I was new to America. And that was only the beginning of the saga.

What I did not know at the time was that those dentists had utterly detached my healthy tooth from its root, and that the tooth was now dying. Why did they do that to my good tooth?

Had they done it on purpose, or was it negligence?

Neither of those possibilities made any sense. Those kinds of mistakes in America seemed incomprehensible. Yet it happened. It was inconceivable to me that my America might fail me.

As a result, for many years, I refused to visit any dentist or seek any treatment for tooth problems. Until one day, as I was biting into a mango, the tooth cracked and fell out of my mouth.

I had nowhere else to go. America was my adopted country now.

7

DURING MY FIRST YEARS IN BEDFORD, I WAS ADDICTED TO THE feeling of freedom that I associated with riding my bike.

On my way home from the library, I used to bicycle through the northern white suburbs of Boston along the Minuteman Bikeway as it connected to the adjacent town of Bedford. As if I were a drifter, I bicycled back and forth between Woburn, Malden, and Bedford.

Birds were chirping as they soared over the lush trees beneath the New England summer sky. After so much trauma, I enjoyed feeling the wind slap my cheeks, watching the glow of stars on moonless nights, and running shirtless in the rain, putting my tongue out to collect the raindrops. Rain, because Somalia is so dry most of the time, is vital and a blessing.

Those were joyful rituals I associated with my life in the Nugaal Valley, living as a nomad with Ayeyo. That was just before the death of my father, before the war.

While I was on the bike and enjoying the greenery and feeling the wind on my cheeks, I crashed into a pole and flipped onto the concrete sidewalk.

I busted my lip, and one of my teeth was chipped. My bicycle was mangled and useless.

Bystanders called the police, and an ambulance came to take me to the local hospital ten minutes away. In the emergency room, they took me into a cubicle right away, but it was more than an hour before someone came in to look at me. Finally, a white doctor stepped in.

"Hi," he said. "Where are you from?"

"Somalia."

"I see you're really skinny. You look a little underweight to me."

I knew enough to understand his language, but my tongue hesitated.

I considered myself a human being. Because I was in his country and he was supposed to be helping me, I thought of him as the best human being possible.

"Have you been in for a medical checkup before?"

"Huh?"

I was still smiling and thinking about his "skinny" comment. I was happy to be skinny because despite malaria and dengue fever, despite a perilous escape through the jungle wilderness and the menace of life-threatening animals, here I was sitting in a fancy hospital with that doctor—skinny, but happy and alive.

"Yeah, I guess I am kind of skinny."

"Have you ever been tested for HIV?"

"What do you mean?" I smiled, not only because of his silly question but because of the way Somali culture viewed HIV or AIDS.

I felt like saying that in my culture and religion, we are bound to practice sexual abstinence. HIV was not part of my cultural experience, since the overwhelming majority of men and women in Somalia practice sex only when they marry. So

HIV just never occurred that often in Somalia. I swallowed my confusion and kept my bloody lips cheerful. I was young, and so was my mind.

"What I'm asking is very simple. Pay attention. Do you have AIDS?"

"No," I said, shocked. "I may be skinny, but I'm totally healthy."

"Fine," he said skeptically. "But you are too skinny to be healthy, in my view."

I was confused. What was he saying? I was in the emergency room for help with an injury, and here he was talking about something else entirely. He numbed my upper lip and gave me a few stitches.

"I'm going to prescribe some painkillers," he said. "But you're going to need to see a dentist."

As the final word of his sentence came out of his mouth, my stomach dropped, and my head pulsed with immediate pain.

"Okay. Thanks."

He sent me home.

I really did not like that doctor. To my way of thinking, he was not a nice person.

Waiting outside the hospital emergency room for my sister to come and pick me up, I sat and considered again the green, trimmed grass, the clean, clear sky, and the cool summer air brushing my cheeks and chin and slipping through my Afro hair.

But I felt something unseasonable, something double-edged and lethal, in the air.

It was my father's dying wish that I study to become a doctor. As I sat there outside the emergency room, waiting, I pictured myself wearing a navy-blue suit with a blue long-sleeved shirt, black leather shoes, and a stethoscope hanging around my neck. I did not think much of the encounter with the doctor, but something in my thoughts was competing and quarreling within me.

My thinking was breaking down and playing havoc. My dad, my father, never said anything to me about the color of my skin.

Now I was on course to make him proud. I spent many hours in the library, lost in books. But my father could not have known about the civil war or my escape to America. He could not have known about those dentists or that white doctor in the emergency room.

A hint of doubt was creeping in as I thought.

The bitter irony I was now forced to confront was that my father's deathbed wish that I become educated, become a physician, could turn out to be dangerous.

These people who thought they were white, who believed, without questioning, certain "facts" about people of color, who carried their privilege, unconsciously or not, deep inside them, they were putting my body in danger.

How could my father have known anything about all that?

In Somalia, as in the rest of Africa, black people are the majority. I never considered skin color a significant factor at all, much less the key factor in whether I lived or died—branded just for wanting to learn, just for wanting to become educated and a professional.

My father's dying wish in Africa could become the death of my future in America.

8

MY THIRD YEAR IN BEDFORD.

Summer was still hanging around, and America was still brand-new to me. I was attending high school and learning quickly, constantly looking around, absorbing everything—the paved roads and manicured grass, the faces of white people jogging or walking with their dogs, the random fire engines or yellow school buses rolling down the road. All those simple things gripped my attention.

My previous life on the run had never allowed me just to relax and enjoy the objects in my surroundings. I was overwhelmed by choices.

One day I was in the school library, thoroughly caught up in a book, when I remembered the five-dollar bill in my pocket and began dreaming about eating a slice of pizza. I grabbed my backpack, stepped out of the library, unlocked my bicycle, and started pedaling, sucking in and breathing out the cool summer air.

Oh, that intoxicating aroma of pizza, french fries, and calzones. I could taste it in the air.

I often passed a local pizza shop on my way to the library, so I pulled up there and leaned my bike against the brick steps.

As I stepped inside, the white man behind the counter raised a large pizza knife in my direction and nodded toward the police station on the other side of the road. "Hey, you! Remember, the cops are right over there!"

I had seen him before, and he had obviously seen me as I bicycled past his shop. But what occupied my mind was the taste of those pizza slices.

"What do you mean?" I said.

"You heard me," he replied.

"Really, I just need two pizza slices," I said in my timid voice, for this was his country, and yet to be mine, and I was just beginning to find my voice in his language.

Deep in my memory lay ingrained the heavy scent of blood, wafting up to my nostrils, so I certainly did not want another conflict in my newly adopted country.

"Here you go," he said, dropping my slices on a plastic plate. "What are you drinking?"

"Nothing," I answered.

I was going to sit there and gobble every morsel of my pizza, but that ominous reference to the police station nearby made me just want to grab my pizza slices and get out of there. I had seen more than enough trouble in my life, and something inside me told me it was better for me to step outside to eat and not linger inside.

That pizza man knew just what he was doing when he said what he said.

He knew the system, America's way of life. He knew all about the police system, the education system, the court system. His remark was conditioned and routine.

I arrived with no country and no friends, a T-shirt, two shirts, two pants, a donated bicycle, a pair of shoes, and a whole lot of regret and heavy remorse that weighed me down. That I had survived the civil war was difficult to deal with. So many had died, so many had been maimed for life. I was lucky. Mama deserved all the credit for saving us as a family. But the thought of how easily life can be taken from you was still upsetting. Death changes you.

Had I done everything I was supposed to do to help others? Why was I spared? What if I failed to live my life to the fullest, the way someone who died might have done? Was I supposed to take their place? How much did I owe the honored dead? Were they looking down on me and judging me?

Even as a child, could I have done more?

There were no answers to those questions, which is why they tormented me, why I couldn't let them go. I thought about death because no one knows what destiny awaits. The unknown was drawing me in. Certainly I was a troubled-looking young man, and the pizza man picked up on it.

I stood outside next to my bicycle and ate my slices alone. As I walked home, pushing my bicycle, I could not stop thinking about that pizza man. Something was eating away at me.

Aren't you supposed to hold your ground against someone who's trying to wrong you or harass you? Shouldn't you stand fast and hold your ground?

What might have happened had that pizza man called the police?

Would they have just arrested me because he felt threatened and called 911? Or would they have felt in their guts the self-evident facts, followed their conscience, and just let me go? Would they have recognized that I was one of them and that I loved America and its green grass, and just let me go home?

When I was confined in that refugee camp, I used to lay my

body down at night on a mat outside, surrounded by trees, grass, and brown sand filled with black and red ants, the air polluted with the drifting scent of feces produced by over thirty-thousand refugees condemned to share a small plot of land.

As I lay on the mat, the stars in the sky became my unreachable playground, bright and dim, large and small. I used to watch the shooting stars as they streaked across the sky. In my mind, there were mother stars, father stars, and children stars.

I loved looking at them so much that often I couldn't wait until the day was replaced by the night and the glow of the stars moved in to take up their places, one after the other.

Lying flat on my back, faceup, I thought that the stars resembled America.

That American star looking down on me from the heavens was no longer so distant.

I was now living in that glowing star.

9

DERIC WALKS TO MY CUBICLE AND PLACES A CUP OF DARK ROAST
Starbucks coffee on the desk. He sits on the chair, places one
of his legs on top of the other, and leans back against the wall.
He seems deep in thought, as if something is bothering him.
During our years together on the job, I have learned to respect
his insight into the ways of white people. He knows them in a
way I do not: he has access to the experience of being a black
man in America. Looking up from my workstation, I take the
coffee he brought me, remove the lid, and take a whiff of it
before sipping. I love the way the aroma of the coffee travels
through my nostrils and into unknown parts of my body.

"Oh," I say. "And it's a grande." Watching him, I hope to
get a reaction, but his gaze seems to pass through me and into
somewhere else, as if he wants to say something to me. It seems
that his lips refuse to obey the commands coming from his
mind. "Are you okay, man?" I ask. His face is blank. His mind
is absent. He continues to sip from his own coffee. His eyes dart
back and forth, frequently looking up at me.

"I'm cool," he responds. His chin gestures in the direction
of the white coworkers sitting in their offices and cubicles, as if
noting that their ears are trained to catch our words.

"Let's go for a walk," I suggest. "You know, I can walk and drink my coffee."

"Let's," he agrees. "We don't belong here."

"I don't know about you," I tease him. "But I know I belong here." In truth, the pain is struggling to rise up inside me.

I remember the day I was circumcised. I was nine years old, and it was a dry day. The local sheikh in our Mogadishu neighborhood grabbed my hand and sat me down under the tree in the open courtyard of our house. As I sat there, he pushed my legs apart, held my penis in his hand, pulled the foreskin back, and marked with ash where he intended to cut. Putting his hand into his burlap bag, he pulled out a sharp, glistening knife and suddenly cut off the foreskin from my penis. The pain then was sharp, but only temporary; here in America, the pain is ongoing.

Standing up from my desk, I take a few steps, extend my hand, grab the door, and hold it open for Deric. He steps out, and I follow him. We walk out, sipping our coffee. The sky remains cloudy, a gloomy day. The grass beneath our feet is wet from the overnight rain. With my light-gray dress shirt sleeves rolled up, I can feel the moist air blowing against the bare skin of my arms. It feels awesome.

"So," I begin. "Now you can tell me what's bothering your soul." Deric appreciates the artistry of my spoken language, and I savor the sincerity of his gaze and the honesty of his words.

"I just have a feeling I may not be working here with you much longer," he confesses.

"What do you mean?"

"I get the sense that, somehow, they're going to fire me."

"What for? You haven't done anything wrong as far as I know."

"Yes, I have."

"What did you do?"

"We're black, aren't we?" he blurts out, his voice breaking.

"So what?" I spit out. "You're trying to say that we've done something wrong, just because we're black?"

"Look, if you really want to survive here, you'd better learn your place and find out who you really are."

After my circumcision, the sheikh threw away the foreskin and then rubbed hot chili pepper into the wounded area. The pain jolted me into manhood, but the look on his face halted my tears. Now, as my departed father used to tell me, I was officially a man, able to endure the miseries of life. In that cultural worldview, where a man is always prepared to wage war and never allowed to cry, I was expected to take the pain. Here in America, I am supposed to show my pain and cry.

It is difficult to find the right words to answer Deric. "Well, you know how I think of you," I say finally.

"What do you mean?"

"I always think of you as my teacher about the real America. What you're saying is real, but this time I think we're going to be just fine, you and me. Hope is real."

"You and that hope of yours," he says. "The hope you're talking about is in the hands of white people." I feel a hint of truth in his words, but I still don't understand what I'm dealing with.

"My break's over." Taking the last sip of his coffee, he walks over to the trash can and throws in the cup. As he takes a few steps back toward his office, I follow. "If I'm even five minutes late, they use it against me," he murmurs to himself. I hear his words, but cannot react.

"You still have a few more minutes," I say.

"Yes, I know," he says. "But I just like to be close to my desk, so I can return on time."

Hope and prayer, I learned from Mama; resilience in the face of threat, I learned from my departed father. Then war naturalized all danger and taught me to tolerate all threats—to the point that I tend to overlook the covert aggressions that to Deric were obvious. My friend was warning me, but I was in denial about the dangers of being a black man in America.

10

DERIC AND I SHARED A HISTORY THAT WENT BACK TO OUR COL-
lege days, when we were both admitted to a university just
outside Boston. I signed up to live in the dormitory, and Deric
chose to take night classes so he could work during the day. For
me, acceptance to college was something magnificent, and the
first day of registration remains vivid in my mind. I headed to
campus in my black Honda Civic with tinted windows, which
I'd purchased after watching the movie *Fast and Furious*. Driving the American highway, I carried deep in my belly nothing
but words of poetry. Wisdom belongs to the learner, for the
learner will know how to fish. Be a learner of life, and a teacher
of the unlearned.

As I walked into the student residence, an older white student greeted me.

"Hiya," he said. "You Boyah?"

He was expecting me. I was on time.

"Yeah, that's me," I said, shaking his hand. "Good to meet
you. I'm glad to be here."

Wearing my red hat backward on my head and a red vest,
a bright Tupac-style chain hanging from my neck, I could not

wait to be part of the college experience. I was still skinny, but I was quite unafraid of what lay ahead.

"I'm Eric," he said. "The resident assistant, or RA."

Eric and I walked together through the revolving door, up the elevator, and down the gray-carpeted hallway to my assigned dormitory room. Eric knocked, and a white boy, my age, opened the door and let us in.

The fall-twilight sun was glowing through the window, and the streetlights were beginning to come on, one after the other. The three of us stood together in that tiny room as Eric said, "Boyah, let me introduce your roommate for the year: this is Brian."

I put out my hand. "Nice to meet you, Brian. My name is Boyah."

Brian looked at me, lowered his gaze, extended his hand, and weakly returned my greeting. If he wanted to hide his discomfort, his cold handshake betrayed him. However, my excitement about starting college like a true American blinded me to the motives behind his hesitation.

Once Eric had handed me the keys, he turned around and left. It was official now: Brian and I were roommates for the year, placed together at random by the college.

Brian was from Alabama, tall and white with blond hair. And I was a skinny black refugee, part African, learning to become a black man.

I counted my steps walking back to the car, as if I were walking on water. I popped open the trunk, threw my backpack over my shoulder, dragged my luggage back to the room, and lifted my backpack onto the bed.

I unzipped my luggage and, taking a couple of steps over to

the closet, hung up my shirts, T-shirts, and jacket. There were two beds right across from each other, two closets separated by a thin wooden wall divider, and two study tables with chairs in the room.

The dying sun flickered in from the window, lighting up the dust that swirled in the air above our beds. I glanced at the closet on Brian's side of the room and noticed three huge gallon bottles of vodka. He also had a stack of CDs in the closet: Metallica, Bob Dylan, Cat Stevens, Black Sabbath, Iron Maiden, Green Day, and David Bowie.

I later became familiar with those performers and learned to like them because they sang about real-life issues. I looked around at Brian's wall posters and noticed in particular one hanging above his bed showing a naked woman, and another of five guys with long, wild hair wearing leopard-print shirts, dark glasses, and bandannas wrapped around their foreheads.

Below that picture was printed the name "Guns N' Roses."

I liked the poster. Brian happened to be listening to their single "November Rain" on his music system. I liked the melody. It entered my ears and ran through my veins, giving me a chill. I loved it! It became one of my favorite songs, in fact.

"Cool," I whispered to myself.

I needed to consider a major. Before he died, my father always wanted me to be a doctor, so when I was in high school I took science classes, thinking I could fulfill his wish for me.

But I despised science class. I hated how the frog we had to dissect smelled. The gore involved in cutting apart that frog reminded me of bullets cutting through human flesh. On the other hand, I excelled in high school math, which did not require much facility with the English language.

My inner being was alienated from math too, but in the Somalia of my childhood, people used to declare that any student who did not excel in math and science was obviously dumb. I felt that I could never reveal my secret love of language and my antipathy for science because I did not want others to look down on me and cast me aside as an intellectually inferior teenager. Nevertheless, I was fascinated by how words turned into sentences, sentences into paragraphs.

Those paragraphs arranged themselves into essays, and those essays eventually became books. Those books could ignite revolution and spread ideas and civilization throughout the world. And I was fascinated by the capacity of words to engender behavior.

Before I came into this world, my journey began with a glance and a timid flickering in the eyes of two young individuals. With an avocado tree separating them, they first uttered two words—perhaps "Sidee tahey" ("Hi"), followed by more glances. More words floated between them, like two rivers merging into each other and then separating.

Few words turned into another: *love*—which sparked intimacy between Mama and Dad.

I was conceived.

When I arrived in America and had to learn English, I was liberated—free to indulge my passion for the art of sentence construction, the complexities of a good story, and the rhythms of soul-searching poetry.

As I went to school and came into contact with Americans who, like me, loved new, interesting words and savored the joys of language, I grew more and more confident. I had survived war and refugee camps, so in America I felt as if nothing could stop me from pursuing the only thing I really wanted out of life: graduation from college. My gratitude for America and its generosity was still limitless.

I would have done anything out of love for America.

I caught myself sitting there and listening to Guns N' Roses and switched my gaze from that vodka bottle to look at Brian, my new roommate for the year. As the music softened my insides, I wondered what destiny had in store for me.

Brian was sitting on the chair, fiddling with something. He saw me look at him, but remained mute. He showed no interest in talking to me.

Months passed, and I made friends with three black guys, Dwaine, Damion, and Kendrick. They lived across campus from me, but we often met up in the cafeteria, where the black students hung out with other blacks, and the white students hung out with other whites. Without thinking consciously, I found myself going to the cafeteria with those three. I was evolving beyond that refugee kid.

I was becoming American. America was teaching me that on American soil I was a black man.

My new friends and I sat together in the cafeteria with plates of bacon and eggs, plastic cups of orange juice, each with our Walkman and our headset hanging on our ears. We listened not only to Tupac Shakur, my personal fave, but also to the other reigning hip-hop acts: Wu-Tang Clan, the Dead Prez, A Tribe Called Quest, Mobb Deep, and the Fugees. Even as we discussed the latest basketball matches, we were comparing the rivalry between Biggie and Tupac with the more current competition between Jay-Z and Nas.

Soon, however, I realized that there was nothing special about living on campus. In fact, it was borderline boring.

Classes usually met Monday to Thursday, so most students

had a long weekend for themselves. It was normal to get drunk: guys would scope out the girls and ply them with drinks. Jealous fights would break out among the boys.

I was still young, so I sometimes took part in the partying, but in my mind I felt as if I were over eighty years old. Indeed, I was a veteran of war. The partying, the drinking, the smoking weed, did not correspond to my dreams. I had something greater and more tangible in mind, for I had buried the corpses of my best friends and comrades in the shallow sands of Africa.

All the while, my roommate, Brian, clearly did not like me very much, and gave the cold shoulder to all my friends. It hurt a bit to know that he was not interested in getting to know me at all.

I had no idea what was going on until late one afternoon I ran into Deric as I stepped out of the dining hall. Since we had no place in particular to go, I thought of something.

"Why don't you come on over to my place, and we can hang out for a while?"

The sky was gray, and snow was falling as we walked together to my dorm.

I was not sure if Brian was in the room, so I knocked on the door. I usually knocked first out of respect because Brian had a girlfriend, and sometimes they were in the room making out. I knocked again. Nothing.

When I knocked once more and still did not hear a thing, I fetched the key from my winter jacket, stuck it in the lock, and turned it. The door opened.

There was Brian sitting on his bed, doing nothing.

"Hey," I said as I stepped in and held the door open behind me for Deric.

"Hey," he replied, lowering his gaze. Deric's glance alternated quickly between me and Brian, taking in everything about the scene as it unfolded.

"Brian, this is my buddy Deric," I said. "Deric, this is my roommate, Brian."

"Hi," Brian said, looking up for a moment and then turning to stare out the window.

Dropping my backpack down on the bed with relief, I removed my shoes and said to Deric, who was still standing in the middle of the room, "Make yourself comfortable."

The trees outside the window were dusted with snow. Over time, I had lost my fascination for snow. I became more wary once I had to drive through piles of it and saw it turn everything white as milk—the cars, the lampposts, the trees, the paved roads, the grass, the buildings.

White is typically associated with power and beauty in America: even angels in heaven are depicted as white. But in Somalia, my mother wore white for my father's funeral and continued to wear white for six months as she mourned my father's departure to the land of the dead.

In Somalia, white is the color of death and mourning.

Deric, at six foot five, was as black as charcoal, with white teeth, and he always carried a blue pick comb in his Afro hair.

As Brian sat and stared out the window, Deric remained standing. I motioned to him. "Sit down."

"Nah, let's get out of here."

"Why?" I said, a little annoyed. "Relax and chill out a bit."

Deric refused, so I relented. Putting on my shoes again, I said, "Okay, let's go."

As we walked back to his car, he looked at me squarely. "Boyah, your roommate is racist."

I was jolted into reality. "What are you talking about?"

"He doesn't like you because you're black."

"I don't know," I said, dubious. "Maybe. He might have been drinking. He's got a big bottle of vodka in the closet. I think he may be an alcoholic."

Indeed, Brian did do a lot of drinking, and I was only just learning how to deal with American bigotry. It was clear from Brian's stubborn silence that something ominous, but foreign to me, was weighing on him.

Overlooking racist behavior or justifying prejudice is never benign, but deadly dangerous. Deric was helping me realize that. I still did not understand that naivete and blind faith in America meant that I was rushing straight into the lion's jaw.

Deric had a history of dancing in the lion's jaw. He knew that racism had to be named and called out. But I was still new to America and, oh, so grateful, indebted to the point of acquiescence.

"If I were you, I'd be careful, buddy," he said with a smirk as we trudged through the snow. "You really shouldn't be around him."

"Well, whatever, man," I said.

For some time, I kept my mouth shut. Then, one night, late in the winter semester, the dam broke.

Brian brought his girl up to our room. They drank cups of vodka together. They giggled, and tickled and teased each other. All the while, I sat on my bed with a headset over my ears and listened to music, pretending not to look at them.

They cuddled on the bed, slipping a hand in each other's pants, whispering and giggling.

Once in a while, Brian or his girlfriend would cast a look in my direction, as if they were waiting for me to get up and leave. But I was certainly not going to be pushed out of my own room.

I threw myself on the bed and lay there thinking. The girl was wearing pink booty shorts under a white Victoria's Secret pajama top.

She was petite, with red hair and a playful kind of beauty. I refused to stay in the room listening to their heavy breathing and watching the movement of their bodies beneath the bedsheets. I was not going to do that to myself.

But now that girl's right breast was exposed, as if she were taunting me.

"Brian, she is not staying in this room!" I bellowed, as rage bubbled up inside me.

I glared at them. Brian ignored me. He didn't respond to me at all.

At that, I got up, grabbed the door, stepped out, and slammed it behind me.

I walked down the hallway, aware of the heaves, the hushes, the sounds of heavy breathing: couples behind the doors were perhaps doing what Brian and his girl were doing in our room. I could hear water splashing, the gurgle of pipes behind the walls, and the strains of music—all different types of music, bass booming from speakers rattling the windows and the sound of student voices climbing up and over their rooms as they belted out their favorite songs. When I heard the strains of "November Rain" in the air again, I stopped at the hallway window, staring out at the falling white snow.

At night, I could distinguish each snowflake under the streetlights, and a single faint smile crossed my lips. Suddenly I was walking in the wintry storm clouds, holding hands and in love, and the image made me forget Brian's snubs and drinking and provocative sex display.

That love song eased my mind. But love is not love unless

it awakens the belly and taps the intestines, and no song lasts forever. Making excuses for Brian's behavior was suffocating.

What purpose was served by my tongue-tied retreat in the face of wrongdoing?

Water from the sky is not only a joy, but a reminder of the drought ahead when the grass turns to gray, the trees wither, birds fall from the sky, and the old drop to their knees in the sand and hold their hands high in prayer. By the time I turned around and went back to the room, the girl was gone, and Brian was alone.

That night, I went to sleep thinking that I needed to remove myself from there. The next morning, I put in a request for a new roommate.

11

BACK WHEN I WAS JUST SEVEN YEARS OLD, DAD SENT ME TO
stay with Ayeyo and learn to live in a harsh environment.
Ayeyo, with my aunts and uncles, was living in the valley of
the Nugaal region in northeastern Somalia.

I remember one day the goats suddenly crying *Meeh*, *meeh*
and *Naa* as they dispersed across the green valley. Ayeyo grabbed
her stick and turned to the dispersing goats. I did not know
what was happening, but she knew that there was a predator
hiding somewhere in the tall grasses. Holding her stick, she
walked about and calmed down the goats. Once the goats and
sheep returned to grazing, Ayeyo came back to me, and I sat
on her lap.

"It was a hyena," Ayeyo said, but I did not see what it was.
That commotion was my first lesson in the forest. Ayeyo's
pointing finger, the gaze on her face, her holding her stick out,
and the laughing hyena behind the sway of tree leaves.

"Where is it?" I asked.

"It saw us and ran off into the forest." Ayeyo walked behind
a goat, hunched down, grabbed one of its rear legs, placed her
head beneath the udder, opened her mouth, and squeezed out
the milk.

"Hahaha." I broke into a smile.

"Now, it's your turn," she challenged me.

But I refused. I kicked the grass and watched a giant gray grasshopper jumping and butterflies hovering. Ayeyo's way of drinking milk was my second lesson. Slowly, I was learning the lessons of living in the wild. As the sun was beginning to rise, I grabbed a goat, held the udder, and squeezed its milk into my mouth. When Ayeyo saw me with milk stains on my cheeks, she let me be, with a grin on her face. I sat there and watched as the goats mixed with the sheep, like white dots over the high and low hills, the wilderness spread out before me like a sheet of green. With a stick in my hand, I walked behind the goats and sheep, slowly strolling into the eye of the rising sun.

"I like this," I whispered, and then I sat cross-legged among the green elephant grass and watched the gray lizards.

"Can you smell the aroma of the camels?" Ayeyo said. "Your nose can always pick up the scent of the camels."

Ayeyo held my hand while she rubbed my head with her other hand. Looking up at her, I sat on her lap.

"I don't see any camels," I said, distracted by all the colorful butterflies hovering in the grass nearby. "Where are they?"

"They're right over there," she said, pointing at distant shapes dotting the vegetation in the mountains. "Those specks are our camels."

Yearning for the day when I would be old enough to care for the camels and become the man Dad wanted me to be, I jumped out of Ayeyo's lap and stood in the grass. Lizards were chasing each other. The sun was climbing, and the trees were standing still. There was a mist in the air. Everything I used to know—buildings, cars, trucks, buses, women, men, children, soldiers with guns, cooking smoke mixed with diesel-engine exhaust—was replaced by wind whistling, rustling grasses, tree branches creaking, birds singing, insects humming, lizards rushing up the tree bark in the calm of the forest. It was Dad's wish to see me, as his first son, hardened by the reality of living without running water or food in the fridge.

Later I watched Ayeyo grab a young goat, slam it into the sand, put her foot on its neck, and cut its throat with a knife. She skinned it and kept the goatskin. I dug a hole beneath a tree, and we buried the goat's stomach. Stretching the goatskin between two poles, Ayeyo left it beneath the scorching sun to dry.

"Do you need the skin?" I still recall asking her.

"Yes," she said. "I'll make it into a water jug and a sleeping mat."

When we were thirsty, our lips dried out, Ayeyo walked over to a hole in a dead tree trunk. It was taller than her reach, so she fetched some dead logs, placed them on top of each other, and climbed up. After she stood on the logs and gawked into the hole, she turned her head to me.

"There's no water in here," she said. She climbed down, placing a hand over her eyes to shield them from the glare of the sun. She took a few steps to another dead tree trunk and climbed up. "Come."

"Okay," I said, running to her.

"Here's some fresh rainwater," she said. "We can drink."

"Sure," I said, even though I had no idea how we were going to get the water out of the hole and drink it.

"We can poke a hole in the side of the tree so the water will pour out," she suggested.

"All right," I agreed. "Let's."

Ayeyo was carrying a gray burlap sack, but I had no idea

what was in it. She climbed down, dropped to her knees in the sand, held the bag, and opened it. She pulled out a knife, a rope, and a water holder made from dried goatskin.

"Keep an eye on the goats," she reminded me.

"Sure," I said. "They're grazing just fine."

"No, watch out," she said. "Predators are always sneaky."

She tied the rope to the water holder and returned to the hole in the hollow trunk. Dropping the jug in the hole and holding the rope, she was able to fetch fresh water. She poured it into her hands, washed her face, and gulped it down while staring at me.

"It's really fresh and tasty," she said, giggling. She handed the jug to me. I took it and drank the same way she did. Sitting on a dead tree trunk, I gazed down at the lush green valley, where our goats grazed beneath the sun. Oh, you see, I belong to the sun, the sand, the tree, and the cold drifting air brushing my skin, and the earth belongs to me. Like a young poet living among his words in the forest, I am becoming a free man. Here in the valley, the art of survival was daily reality, and I was learning fast.

I hit a gray lizard with my stick and cut off its tail. I stepped on ants and grasshoppers and held butterflies in the palm of my hands. Giggling, I returned to where Ayeyo sat under an acacia tree. I saw a gray scorpion crawling toward her, and I whammed it with my stick once, twice, and then stepped on it.

"You're so brave," she said, holding her stick in between her legs.

I beamed, but before I could open my mouth to say something, I saw wild monkeys coming down from the hills. Our goats panicked. Standing upright, my chin up, I held my stick high and ran out of the shade. Ayeyo followed me. The monkeys stood their ground as they toyed with us and probed our defenses. They pretended to run, but stopped, giggled, and stamped their feet. But we were not afraid of them. The monkeys were hunting the kid goats for food, so all we had to do to defend the little ones was stretch out our hands, strike our sticks on the trees and in the grass, and scream, "Get away!" The land was teaching me to be brave, and as long as Ayeyo was not afraid, I stood there and beat with my stick, pretending to be fearless as a lion cub. I was to become part of the land and live as its inhabitants lived, roaming about looking for something to eat, or fetching water beneath a mountainside somewhere.

The colony of monkeys dispersed: some scattered on the hillside, some lay in the grass, others played at the edge of the nearby mountains. With my stick drawn, I sat on top of an anthill. I watched the monkeys, but they too watched me. Cool air tickled my face. As far as my eyes could see, there was nothing but a vast land with elephant grass, hills, cliffs, and random tall trees where the green forest merged with the blue sky. And beyond it, sheep and goats as far as the eye could see, wild horses grazing on the hills, jackals sitting on rocks, lizards sticking their heads out from their holes beneath the anthill—all bathing beneath the eye of the sun in the valley. Oh. The sun. The creatures of the valley need it. The rays of the sun connect us all. Beneath the sun, we are one colorful creature. Happiness is everywhere.

Anthills, mounds of earth formed by ant colonies when they dig and construct their underground nests, were always part of my forest playground. Anthills can rise as tall as ten feet, but the one I played on that day was four feet tall and just as wide. Gray lizards moved up and down the anthill. Chasing them, I watched them disappear into their holes beneath the anthill. Climbing on top of the hill, I stood there, placed both hands on my hips, and stared down at Ayeyo looking up at me.

I climbed the anthill and then jumped, then climbed back up and jumped again. The sound of my laughter rose and mixed with the sound up above in the air: the tree branches swaying and slapping into each other, the howl of the monkeys hopping over the bushes, the tread of the goats stepping through the grass, the whistle of the birds, all the sounds made by unknown species in the unknown forest.

From the top of the anthill, I watched the monkeys jump around as they chased squirrels, rabbits, and lizards. Beyond the monkeys, an ostrich walked leisurely with her young.

"Hahaha." I smiled.

"You come down now," Ayeyo said.

I jumped down hard, but instead of landing on my feet, my face hit the grass: I cut my lower lip, and my nose bled. I felt dizzy and briefly passed out. As I lay at the bottom of the anthill, I felt the tiny legs of ants crawling on the skin under my shirt. Ayeyo stood over me, grabbed my hand and pulled me up, but my legs became numb, and I could not get up. Later that evening, my lips cracked with tiny cuts. My forehead sweated with fever. Tears gushed from my eyes. I was sick.

A new day had begun for me. Ayeyo knelt down in prayer and placed her forehead on the ground once, twice. Then, as she murmured her prayers, she drew the palm of her cupped hands closer to her mouth, blew blessing air into them, and rubbed her hands on my body. Ayeyo brought a jug of water. She removed my T-shirt and shorts and washed me with the water we could not spare. After the bath, Ayeyo gave me a cup of milk, wrapped me in a shawl around her hip, and sang to me,

Huuwaa yeey huuwaa. When you were born and first cried.

She held me in her lap and rubbed my hair.

Huuwaa yeey huuwaa. Oh, perfect child, you're from the finest, deep roots.

Then she placed a wet towel on my forehead.

Huuwaa yeey huuwaa. Oh, perfect child, you're the son of a tall and slim father.

Her melody lifted up and mingled with the singing birds before entering my ears.

Huuwaa yeey huuwaa. Your father took his shoes.

She held me on her chest and wrapped her hands around me.

Huuwaa yeey huuwaa. Your father left, and we do not know if a nomad got him.

I opened my eyes and showed my teeth, but the pain refused to dissipate.

Huuwaa yeey huuwaa. We do not know if he will come back safe.

Pacing, Ayeyo held me on her hip and walked around, still singing and clicking her tongue.

Huuwaa yeey huuwaa. Oh, perfect child, you are as handsome as the horizon.

Taking steps back and then forth, she hummed and whistled.

Huuwaa yeey huuwaa. The poetry of the landscape will man you up, my child.

The forest in the valley whistled. I contracted polio in that valley where I came against every adversity, every antagonist.

12

THE MORNING WHEN I OFFICIALLY BECAME A HIGH-SCHOOL
student is etched in my memory in permanent marker. I wore a
white shirt, khaki pants, and white Adidas shoes.

As I got off the yellow school bus and walked through the
doors of the high school, the principal, my school counselor,
and my new ESL teacher were all waiting to welcome me.

As a newly arrived, skinny African boy, it was hard to believe that three white people were waiting there just to welcome me. I found it difficult to close my lips, and my cheeks
spread like elastic. I felt I was a bird flapping my wings just
above the clouds. My feet were on the ground, but my being
was flying above somewhere, happy.

"Do you see that?" The principal pointed upward with his
finger toward a row of flags, just above the portrait of a man
wearing a bushy beard and mustache with a pointy nose and
flat cheeks. Joyful smiles kept my lips occupied, and I could not
do anything else.

I was so elated. My stomach felt like paws of kittens were
walking through my intestines.

"That's the Somali flag," the principal remarked.

As my eyes followed his gesture, I saw the Somali flag. "You are Somali American."

He confirmed for me the words I wanted to hear, the words I had been waiting for.

"I am Somali American," I repeated.

Despite the fact that I was still struggling to master English, the school placed me in regular courses. All the students were white, except for those few black students bused in from the inner city. Since I belonged to neither group, I walked everywhere alone and sat in the classroom alone. It was impossible to hide from every wondering gaze the fact that I was a skinny black African boy. As I walked through the hallways of the school carrying a backpack and wearing an oversize shirt, my spirit wished that I had been born in America, rather than in Somalia. Students and teachers alike frequently stopped to ask me about Africa and my life there and seemed genuinely fascinated whenever I opened my mouth to tell them how I got to the United States and ended up in Bedford. If I liked a girl, I might take a notion to talk to her. But I felt that if I tried to talk to her, my words would need to sound pleasing to her. And since I did not know the language or the culture very well, I kept to myself, with only my imagination for companionship.

During those magical years, my America was everything to me, and I walked everywhere with that dream in front of me. My name appeared once in a while in the local town newspaper, the *Minuteman*, because I'd made the high-school honor roll. Still, it was difficult to make friends and get close to people.

In Somalia it always seemed that as soon as I got to know someone, they died. That hurt.

One of my classmates asked me whether I went around naked in Africa. I never took offense at questions like this; I was hungry for acceptance and for a home to belong to and a country to claim. To my way of thinking, I was nothing and had nothing here in suburban white America, and I was looking for friends.

In one class, my white teacher seemed to keep staring at me somehow. As our eyes met, I looked the other way. As my gaze turned back to her, I kept seeing her studying my face. I knew she saw me as exotic, different.

"We respect all cultures," the teacher announced. "Along those lines, I have a question I just have to ask you, Boyah. Have you ever eaten monkey meat?"

The other students in the class turned on a dime in my direction, waiting for me to respond. Something ripped me up inside my stomach.

"No way," I said emphatically, combating her foolish question with my sincerity. "In Somalia, we only eat chicken, goat, camel, and lamb."

I'm sure she could see from my demeanor how uncomfortable she was making me. All the students' eyes locked on me, and my face was soaked with sweat. My armpits itched, but I reminded myself that no words could hurt me the way bullets in war could.

She was determined to pursue the point and justify herself. "I've seen scientific reports on television," she said piously. "How HIV got started because some Africans regularly eat monkey meat as part of their jungle diet."

I wanted to correct her in no uncertain terms and teach her a lesson in human dignity, but the English language belonged to me only partially.

In any case, words were limited in their usefulness at this point, even as the danger to my sanity was increasing. That American star looking down on me from the heavens was now no longer so distant. I was living in America, and America was becoming my teacher, teaching me something different about that glowing star.

What made the day more memorable was that when I left the class, I went to the gym. I was skeletal, but I liked the image of boys my age with their biceps protruding, and I was thinking that perhaps I could become more American if I were to have some muscles. I could become rugged, masculine, and tough, like Rambo. In Somalia, self-defense in war is the very definition of male beauty, so it did not take much for me to see in Rambo the perfect image of America.

Walking through Bedford, I imagined myself a guerrilla fighter, carrying a sword, a kukri knife, and a gun, cutting down all the killers I encountered in my Somali childhood.

At other times, I was nothing in my mind but a refugee with no friends or country of my own. At those moments, I felt naked in front of the world, like a beggar with no dignity.

That was the me who went to the gym that afternoon after class.

I saw other boys from my class remove their shirts and pump their muscles. Inspired by what I saw, I proceeded to take off my own shirt and grab two twenty-five-pound dumbbells. As I struggled to raise them in each hand, my ears detected a titter of laughter coming from a corner of the gym.

I hesitated and stood still, holding the weights. Muffled laughter ricocheted throughout the gym like a burst of bullets. I dropped the weights. Finding my image in the gym mirror, I saw the bare bones of my chest reflected back at me. Oh, shit, I thought, a hint of embarrassment crawling somewhere beneath my skin.

That was the moment when I knew I was done with the idea of developing muscles as a way to define myself in America. I resolved to read and understand something about the world and then to write about it—not for the world's sake, but for my own understanding.

I was certainly not a monkey eater, but I was also no longer an impersonator of some make-believe American hero.

13

I MET DERIC MY JUNIOR YEAR IN HIGH SCHOOL. MY FAMILY HAD moved to a different town, and I began to attend a new high school. I remember that it was during lunch in the overcrowded high-school cafeteria. I was sitting with friends, and Deric was eating lunch at the table in front of me. Holding a mouthwatering cheeseburger with onions, pickles, tomato, lettuce, and ketchup and mayonnaise oozing out the sides, he was eating leisurely. I picked up my own burger and held it up to my mouth, but before I could take a bite, I noticed one of the white kids—we knew him as Shotgun—sitting down at our table. I had been looking for him. He had been bullying my younger brother, once, twice, three times, and each time he got away with it. Shotgun was feared by everyone; he was one of the school-bully boys with protruding biceps. Often wearing aviator shades with fancy hats, he walked with style.

The other kids still thought of me as some kind of weird African kid with a gimpy leg. Usually when they picked fights with each other, I considered them silly and somewhat naive because I had seen real gunfights, bullets penetrating bodies, breaking bones, and sending many souls down below the soil.

I had witnessed the murder of loved ones; I was not like them. But bullying my brother was something I could not tolerate.

Shotgun looked over at me, and I put my burger down and stared back at him.

"Look," I said. "You need to learn to leave my brother alone."

"So, what's up?" he shot back. "You think you're going to do something, nigger?"

"What did you say?"

"You heard me," he said, raising his hand, showing off to all the boys sitting at our table.

I lost it, and something snapped. I picked up my tray, with my hamburger and all my lunch, and threw it in his face. Then I jumped over the table and punched him. Everyone dispersed. I thought he would fight back, but I struck him so suddenly that he was utterly dazed and disoriented. The school security man ran over to pull me off him and lead me to the principal's office, where I was given a five-day suspension. I did not know it at the time, but Deric had been watching.

This was the beginning of our bonding; after that Deric started to tease me regularly. Whenever I saw him in the hallway, he would joke, "Man, you sure are crazy. You fight like some kind of African bushman."

"You can get lost and get out of my face," I would reply in kind.

The other kids thought I was crazy for fighting Shotgun. "What the hell happened to his leg?" one kid asked his friend.

"Ask him," he said sarcastically. "Maybe it's an African thing."

I knew they were teasing, so I shot back, "Do you know what happened to my leg?"

"No," he said. "Tell me."

"A round of bullets from an AK-47 hit my leg," I said to him.

"Really!" He appeared shocked.

"Yeah," I said. "Those bullets took half of my leg."

"Word!"

"I'm so sorry," one of his friends murmured.

As I walked away, I heard him say, "He's a badass."

"He really does come from Africa, doesn't he?" another kid said.

"Yeah. Don't mess with him!"

From that point on, as I limped around the school, my classmates either stared at me or greeted me as if I were a badass African warrior with battle scars. I had, in fact, learned the ways of a nomadic warrior in the Nugaal Valley. But because I lied to my classmates that I had been shot in the leg during combat, my fight with Shotgun would be the first and last fight of my high-school career.

14

I was still skinny, but I wore T-shirts and jeans like any other American.

Once I noted how girls flocked to guys who owned cars, and figured out that no girl would talk to me as long as I was still riding my bike and taking the bus to school, I got a job at a local gas station and worked as many hours as possible. Once I got my license and saved enough to buy a car, I began visiting used-car auctions all over the state of Massachusetts until I found just the right car for me.

A red car, my favorite color.

One spring afternoon, just before graduation, I needed to take a break from schoolwork, and decided to just drive around and let off some steam before retreating back to the library. Making my way through the revolving doors and down the stairs to the parking lot, I greeted the homeless black guy living beneath the bridge.

Then I climbed into my red Chevy Malibu with a CD changer, a speaker box in the trunk, and a modified exhaust system made to sound better and louder. The custom-made low-hanging suspension my car sported made for better gravity performance.

When I bought my Chevy Malibu lowrider, it already had all those modifications, and I liked it because I desperately wanted to fit in and be an American.

I wanted to eat, talk, walk, shop, dance, date, and drive like Americans.

Not like all Americans, but like those Americans with rhythm and style and blazing poetry behind their music. With all four car windows rolled down halfway, I was driving along leisurely, listening to Tupac's "Hail Mary."

Tupac's lyrics of resistance—his boldness and bravery and pride in his history—touched me deeply and were becoming part of me. The word battles in his rap were not something new to me; in my early teen years in Somalia, when I was a man in the making, I used to memorize poetry and proverbs to use in word battles with the other boys on the school playground. In Somalia, language is everything, and everyone uses poetic language in daily speech. In my boyhood Somalia, a brave man with brave words was the beginning of handsomeness. In Tupac's music, I heard an echo of the language games I grew up with, a reverberation in English of everyday conversation in Somali, the poetry of war and honor and dignity I used to listen to and try to recite.

Tupac's art was something I understood viscerally.

During my childhood wandering through the Nugaal Valley, words were everything. In the afternoon, when the yellow sun fell, we gathered and drank our tea with words. We welcome our births with words. We bless our weddings with words. We even bury our dead with words. Spoken metaphors and sung proverbs ruled my childhood in the Nugaal Valley.

Words with rhythm and cadence might help me avoid physical altercations with other boys; but more important for me at the time, words with tempo and rhyme had the potential to make that girl I had a crush on turn her head and take notice.

As I drove along, my head was bobbing up and down to the beat, and the clouds overhead were perfect, like an artist's best work. I was reminding myself of how I came to this country, stepping off the plane in a pair of secondhand Adidas, a Hawaiian shirt, and knockoff Ray-Ban aviator sunglasses. Everything I owned, I carried in a plastic bag stamped with the logo of the International Rescue Committee.

Nowadays, I thought, here you are, wearing your best suits, putting on your favorite colognes, driving the streets of a Boston springtime in your classic Chevy with the windows rolled down. The CD player switched to the R&B cut "All That I Am" by the American singer Joe. The weather was soothing, and the sun was neither hot nor cold.

The road ahead was clean and clear. The green grass on each side of the road was perfectly trimmed, as if just given a fresh haircut. It was a numinous day, and there was something radiant rising within me in the power of that song, in the notion of a man in love, in the miracle of the day.

I was feeling my soul soar up and over the clouds, and up there I danced in my dream with a pretty angel with a thin waist and a carved face.

That pretty angel was not living in the clouds. She was in another town. In my car, I was driving on those surging waves of music to pick her up. My face was washed in the cool, wafting air, and my nose below her right ear was picking up the magical enchantment of her natural scent, mixed with her favorite Cool Water perfume.

My softening heart was skipping a beat. My arms were wrapped around her.

"Stop the car, you son of a bitch!"

I heard the words lunge from a passing police cruiser.

"Stop the car, I said, you filthy son of a bitch!"

I reached for the volume knob and turned the music down.

Again: "Stop the car right now!"

The police cruiser had pulled up beside me, and I saw a white cop glaring at me.

I turned the music off completely. My mind abruptly dropped down from the clouds into America. By this time, I understood better the very real danger posed by police.

"Pull the goddamned car over right now!"

We were side by side. He was on the left-hand side of the double yellow lines. He was shouting through his open passenger window.

I pulled over and turned off the engine. He parked behind me. I saw his flashing police lights in my rearview mirror.

Reaching for the glove compartment, I pulled out my registration. Putting my hand in the back pocket of my pants, I took out my wallet. With my license and registration in hand, I watched him climb out of the cruiser and walk slowly toward me.

One of his hands was on his radio, the other on his weapon.

As he drew closer—veins bulging and face contorted—he looked like he had just found out I was sleeping with his wife. Black people knew not to drive through white neighborhoods, and I had been told not to, but I did it anyway.

You see, your perspective in life sometimes gets you into trouble. The war in Africa did not kill you because it was not your time to die, and your feeling this late afternoon is that some cop in a uniform will stop you only if that is your destiny for that afternoon. Yet your death is real.

Your health and sickness, dentists and doctors, are real. God is real.

And you always need to remind yourself that destiny is real.

You need to be *careful* that the conflict and warfare down through generations in America do not suffocate you as they will George Floyd or shoot you as they will Ahmaud Arbery. The anger and the brutality of this cop does not belong to him; it belongs to America.

There is nothing deceptive about any of this. Yes, look up your history and read it.

"Sorry, Officer," I said, wiping my face with my hand. "Whatever I did wrong, I'm sorry." I was sure that I had followed all the traffic lights and kept the speed limit because I was only cruising along, driving slow and smooth, like Joe's transformative words and the feelings of love they evoked in me.

"Hand over your license and registration, you piece of shit," he barked.

His fury was totally beyond my comprehension. The anger in his words, however, couldn't touch me, and I remained calm.

In that other distant land, I had seen mouths gasping for their last breath, and I had heard the peculiar sound of an old man sobbing. I had witnessed a broken widow standing over the lifeless body of her husband, and lived to offer her words of consolation. At that moment, I was grateful for the patience I could draw from the reservoir of pain gathered in my memory.

Still, I had yet to understand why he was cussing me out.

"Just who do you think you are, anyway?"

"I'm not sure what I did wrong, Officer," I said, trying to defend myself.

My heart had begun humming with a tiny fury of its own. This white man was acting like an aggressor. Reverting to that nomadic resistance culture I learned in the Nugaal Valley, I found myself thinking that a real man with such an impressive uniform should not be preying on the powerless. A real man protects the weak and fights for the valley, guards the herd, shields the land from spoilers and polluters and from those who would harm those living in the land.

This white man in a uniform, I thought, was just itching to do something to me, to threaten me with some harm. I wished I could just grab him by his uniform collar, yank him across the ocean, and drop him off in the middle of the war raging in my rearview memory.

This police officer is pathetically frail, I kept thinking. But a weak man with a gun is dangerous.

In that moment, I was determined not to allow him to get the better of me and outmaneuver my destiny. I was born for this, it seemed to me: I could not be defeated or broken.

"You failed to stop for a pedestrian," he snarled, snatching the license and registration from my hand. "Listen, I'm going to find out who gave you this license, asshole."

He returned to his vehicle to put my name into his computer and sift through for anything he could use against me, all the while cursing and swearing.

Remember, I said to myself, you are in the heart of Boston, a liberal city, a historic American city with fancy schools and people wearing T-shirts and caps bearing the names of their favorite New England sports teams and jogging and biking and reading books in the cafés.

But you are black, I told myself, and now America is teaching you that you are black. You're a naturalized American, not born here. You have a funny name and speak with an accent. Moreover, you're driving a fancy Chevy Malibu with a popping red color in an exclusively white neighborhood. Remember the first rule you learned in high-school English: you need to show, not tell, the story. These liberal white people in Boston are trained never to tell you that they are racist, that they are inclined to cut open your invisible soul without a sound.

But when the attack comes, everything you know, you question.

Everything you believe, you doubt. Everything you think is rendered meaningless.

You run out of options; everything goes wrong. You get sick and just break down and cry. You see yourself mirrored in the ones the cops murder.

However innocent you may be, you are not confident.

America is making you a black man.

I stared at him strutting back to me.

"Mm-hmm," I hummed to myself.

He opened his teeth, and pure fire spewed out. "What the hell are you doing around here?" He lowered his head to my eye level, shoving his face nearly nose-to-nose with mine, unsettling me, filling the small space between us with a palpable sense of menace and personal danger. "This doesn't seem like your kind of neighborhood."

"Just driving through," I said coolly, holding my nerves. "On my way to the next town." I gave him no inkling of the fury stirring in my spirit. "I'm not questioning you, sir, but really, I didn't see anyone crossing the street." As I was speaking, I could see he was busy looking at the gold leather car seats. All four windows were still half down. "I would have stopped."

"Here," he said, handing back my license and registration. "You can go. But don't let me catch you in this town again. You hear me? I don't stutter. Never again, boy."

"Thank you, Officer," I said politely, tossing my license and registration onto the passenger seat. Then I began to feel the effects of his vulgar white language.

"Fuck him!" I muttered under my breath. He made a U-turn and sped away, but I continued saying to myself, "Fuck that asshole!"

Hitting the engine, I drove away in silence. Soon cool air brushed my face, making my Afro shiver. A smile crossed my lips, and the tension and fury I was feeling began to lift.

I was no longer the naive African immigrant. I was becoming a black man, an American learned in the ways of the American people, conscious of the danger all around me.

In Africa, the perpetual possibility of assault had shaped my childhood worldview and regulated the kinds of choices I made. I had learned to dance with terrorizing aliens besieging and destroying my existence. War invaded my home and turned my childhood playground into dust in the wind. Guns took away the young girl who was my childhood crush and dispatched her soul up into the land of the dead, beyond the sky.

Artillery had invaded and bulldozed my school to the ground. Famine had invaded my belly in those putrid refugee camps. And now America was invading my consciousness, making me into a snake-charming dancer. It was this dance that enabled my escape.

From this racist, psychopathic cop.

Unharmed.

Unscathed.

15

ONE MORNING IN SOMALIA.

The soil was dry, and the sun was scalding.

I stepped out of the abandoned two-room house in which my mother and my six younger siblings and I were squatting as refugees. I went to meet up with my friend Omar, and we held hands and walked aimlessly together through that city of war and bloodshed where women and children living in a metropolis of shallow graves refused to cry, their wails stuck in their throats. Their faces dry and wrinkled. Their hair wild. Their bellies empty. Their death close.

I heard a sound like "Grrrr."

Turning to Omar, I asked, "Is that your stomach?"

"Yeah," he replied. "I can hear yours rumbling too."

We knew that we had no way to get food and no way to find peace. We couldn't help each other. We were drifters in pain and dancers with death.

As we strolled together, the hungry growls from our bellies mingled with the cracking report of machine guns and random artillery fire and rocket-propelled grenade guns lifting up over the city and agitating the birds. We had grown accustomed to the sound of weapons. And because we considered ourselves not boys but men in the making—real men, but without guns—neither of us flinched. We thought that men were not supposed to cry. Once provoked, real men get even with the enemy.

Death was close to us; it was our companion.

As we continued our walk, a classic light-blue four-door Mercedes-Benz halted near us. Four men with pistols and AK-47s stepped out of the vehicle and then dragged from the car two young men dressed in green army fatigues.

Omar suddenly reacted. "Oh, shit," he said. He pointed at the car. "They're gonna kill those guys."

We saw the men with guns cock their weapons as they cornered their two prisoners at the side of the road. We were near enough that we could hear them speak.

"What's the holdup?" one of the men yelled. "What are we waiting for?"

Before anyone could react, they sprayed the two men with bullets and then turned and climbed back into the vehicle. The Mercedes spun its wheels and vanished. One of the victims was dead, the other still breathing, writhing.

Random people walked by. Some stopped to look, but no one helped. Omar and I looked at each other for a moment and then joined hands again and continued walking. There was nothing for us to say; death and dying lived inside us.

Minutes later, Omar stopped walking and released my hand.

"We should pray," he said solemnly. Dropping to his knees on the side of the road and facing east toward Mecca, he gestured to me to do the same. I did as he asked.

Our bent knees resting in the soft sand and our hands cupped together, we raised our faces upward in the direction of God, and our lips began to move in silent prayer. In war, you are either dead or alive—that's all that counts.

"Dear God," Omar intoned emotionally. "We welcome whatever death is our destiny."

Indeed, it was not fear of death that caused us to fall to our knees, and we did not think to pray for food, peace, or prosperity. We prayed for a quick and painless death.

"When the time comes for us to die, please don't make us suffer on some roadside."

Omar was thinking what I was thinking: we accepted our fate and knew we must die, but we did not want to suffer. That wounded man gasping in the soft sand was an apocalyptic image, but death would ease his pain.

Death in war is only short-term pain. The suffering and death inflicted by white people in America are long-term, and worse. Their small-minded bigotry produces continuous injury to your body. You cannot sleep. You cannot eat. You cannot talk. You no longer care about yourself.

You're afraid of the cops. Fear follows you around. Moreover, you cannot touch the source of your pain. You cannot think clearly. You cannot earn a living. You cannot get up and take a walk without feeling invisible pain.

Such injury takes you prisoner. Your body becomes a residence for high blood pressure and diabetes. Nothing belongs to you. No one knows about your injury. You become a perfect candidate for COVID-19 to take your body to the land of the dead.

As a child, faced with the possibility or certainty of death in war, I never lost any sleep. But my experience in America made me an insomniac.

Whenever you try to talk to white people about race, about racism and its effects, they quickly change the subject because their conscience is fragile. In Somalia, I knew of two militia fighters who killed innocent women and children, burned down entire villages, and destroyed livestock and houses during the civil war with no justification. One of them escaped to the United States, but the memory of his many crimes he could not outrun or evade.

Now, here in the white streets of America, he lives homeless, an alcoholic. He holds out a cup, begging drivers and pedestrians.

The other renegade is still in Somalia. Since he was a childhood neighbor and acquaintance, when I had the opportunity I visited him in the compound of a madhouse where he still lives today, chained to a tree root, a filthy green sarong soaked in urine and feces wrapped around his waist. His front teeth are chipped away, and his lips are cracked, oozing blood. Zigzagging scars mark his sunken cheeks, and dried tears congeal beneath his eyes. His body tells the story of his victims.

Two lost souls.

Two broken spirits.

America is on the path of those two broken souls, who were responsible for maiming and killing without any justification. Once you do that, you are looking into the face of your own demise and sitting on the edge of destruction.

Your conscience cannot carry the weight of your crimes against Elijah McClain as he walked home from the store, Michael Brown as he was out buying cigarettes, Ahmaud Arbery as he jogged in the neighborhood, Breonna Taylor as she slept in her own house—all lynched.

And then there are those countless other innocents who were not so lucky as to be on television. When you wrong others, your conscience turns rotten. The effect of those crimes does not go away. It lives on in the consciousness of those who draw down the bequest and participate in the legacy. White people in America cannot simply run away and change the subject, for the luxury of a green suburban lawn will not ensure safety.

That legacy of poisoned black blood and screams of horror leaves its mark upon the crime-ridden conscience of white Americans and will, in time, carry them off either to destitution or to the madhouse.

"Amen," Omar intoned, when we had finished praying.

"Amen," I whispered.

16

ONE DAY AT THE OFFICE.

When lunchtime comes, Deric and I, as usual, are eating chicken cutlets and sipping cans of Coke. Something is heavy on his mind that he wants to bring up with me, but we usually do not have time because we have to work.

Beyond the windows, snow is falling. The sky is gray.

"I called in sick again," he explains.

In my mind, I repeat the word *sick* rhythmically. I am sick too, but I cannot reveal that to him. Yes, Americans discuss such things. I remember my father lying on a stripped mat, wheezing in total pain, eyes weeping silently, but I never heard him complain or say a word to anyone about his sickness. My lips too remain sealed for now.

"Really?" I say.

"Yes, I had to," he says, as if white oppressors lurking in the shadows are even now hovering over him. "Fuck them, I need to take care of my own health!"

Deric coughs and sneezes over and over. Even confessing his agony triggers symptoms.

"Yeah, you still sound sick to me."

"Man, everything is making me sick. First, work. And now

my cat's dead." He sneezes. "Everything about the job I'm do-ing is being monitored, and I just don't know what to do. I like this job, and I really don't want to lose it."

"If it's destined for you to keep this job, you will. Nobody can alter that."

"You and your destiny talk, man. In this country, the des-tiny of the black man is in the hands of the white people."

"I understand," I say. "You and I will get through this to-gether."

"I can't take this anymore." He cries out softly, and his voice turns scratchy. "But I need to work, so I can afford to pay my rent."

"I hear you, man. I might come from a different culture, but our pain is the same."

"You're a strong brother," he says. "I don't know anything about how it is in Africa, but over here they really treat black folk bad."

"Ah," I say, smiling against the hurt. "I come from a nomadic family of fighters. Those racists will never see me give in."

"We'll see about that." He smiles to himself ruefully. "This American race war will crush even someone hardened like you."

Deric's warning hits me like falling cement, as if an enemy were gathering at the gate. But unlike in real war, there is no enemy actually visible at the gate. Invisible and evasive, this enemy is more lethal to me than the real experience of war lying dormant in my memory.

During my youth in Somalia, war was something tangible, something you could see and confront. But here in America, to my complete surprise, I have found the enemy to be clandes-tine, penetrating but intangible. I refuse to submit, but Deric is hurt. He is wounded. And right now, sitting in front of me, Deric begins to weep.

Oh, no, I say to myself. What in the world can make a grown man cry like this?

I don't understand. Why should a dead cat so alter Deric's consciousness that he breaks down emotionally? Growing up in Africa, I never witnessed a grown man weep, much less weep over a dead cat or some other domestic animal like a dog, goat, sheep, or pigeon. In my nomadic childhood culture, so deeply embedded in my spirit, death cannot and should not be able to stir up the emotions of any man, let alone make him weep.

Deric grew up confined to public housing in the hood, just a few towns away from here, with a basketball court, Taco Bell, and a playground. I, on the other hand, grew up free in a broad valley filled with goats, camels, sheep, and forest animals. Every inch of that valley I used to claim as my playground, and I was afraid of nothing.

That was the Somalia of my childhood. Now, here in America, I am not comfortable with a crying man, let alone a large man like Deric crying.

Deric wipes his tears away. "Trust me, they will break your spirit too."

"Man, come on. Forget that, okay?" I gather up my trash. "Let's head back. I gotta go back to work." I glance at my watch. I still have thirty minutes left for lunch. Perhaps my body is refusing to confront the pain of a difficult conversation, my best friend weeping in front of me.

On the way down the hallway toward our office, we stop to peer out a window. Snow is falling harder and harder.

It feels like an omen.

17

BY THE TIME MY SENIOR YEAR OF HIGH SCHOOL CAME ALONG, I was still pumping gas at a local gas station. The winter before, I'd almost died pumping gas because my white manager refused to allow me to come inside, even when there were no vehicles to service.

Even in the middle of a snowstorm, he insisted I stand outside next to the gas pump for a full eight-hour shift. I needed the money pumping gas to finance my car and help pay the rent, so I persevered and kept my pain in my belly.

One day early in the year, the academic counselor called me into his office.

"Have a seat," he said, gesturing in front of him. "How are you doing?"

"Fine."

"Are you thinking about applying to colleges?"

"No," I lied. I wanted to go to college, but I didn't know how.

He nodded. "That's great. Get a job and go to work."

"I'm already working at a gas station."

"What do you do there?"

"I pump gas. But I hate it, especially during the winter."

"Hey," he said, pointing at me. "Remember you're making

money. Life is all about making money." He paused. His expression was utterly serious. "Perhaps you can pick up another job. With two jobs, you can get some experience and earn even more income."

I already knew something about this man. He had advised my younger sister to get a job and suggested she might be better suited to raising kids. My younger brother, he'd counseled to apply to truck-driving school. Offering black students dead-end career advice seemed to be his standard practice, and all the black students used to talk about it regularly. By this time, I was a reader. I knew his kind through books like James Baldwin's *The Fire Next Time* and Eldridge Cleaver's *Soul on Ice*.

I told my mother all about it.

"Boyah, don't listen to him," she said. "He doesn't belong to our kin, we don't expect him to protect us, so he can't be trusted. And we're not any of his kin either, so don't pay him any attention."

"Mm-hmm," I hummed.

"Whatever those teachers or counselors are saying to you is not the final word in life, understand? You listen to them respectfully because you have to, but afterward you must discard their words."

I was listening carefully.

My mother came to America with nothing but her words, and Mama was a master wordsmith. During our struggle to escape the war, we were constantly on the move, looking for anywhere we could find peace, water, and food. Time and time again, Mama's skill at verbal repartee saved us from death and injury. When her words danced, they subverted the minds of man-killers. Once during the civil war, six militia soldiers, armed with AK-47s and knives, broke down the door where we were hiding and lined us up against the wall, ready to rob and kill us. Mama went eyeball-to-eyeball with them and led them to think we were not worth their bullets. In the end, they turned around and left. The words from her mouth had set us free.

I learned to obey Mama's words, and carry them with me.

"We are guarded by our culture and belief in God," she'd say. "Because of that, we survived the war and made it to America. Now, I expect all of you to finish high school and go on to enroll in a university. The worst is behind us—remember that. And now that we are here, all of you will go on to college. That is my wish."

Her words to me in rhythmic Somali became my bulwark.

The Somali language is unique in its use of figurative language and poetic devices. Poetry and proverbs characterize the everyday conversation of adult Somalis, and for that reason anthropologists call my birthplace "the nation of poets." I am part of an ancient people with an ancient culture in which poetry animates the language of everyday life, like food and tea or breathing air.

Poetry is inscribed in daily life, and conversation in Somali naturally falls into rhythm and meter. Moreover, metaphor is used by everyone, all the time. Every day Somalis judge you by the quality of imagery you use, by how lyrically, how skillfully, you deploy the language, how intelligently and artistically you express yourself. Those qualities determine how much respect you earn from the rest of the community. Being a bad poet is the worst crime you can commit when conversing in Somali, and there is no worse humiliation than when you must lower your gaze, rebuffed for using words judged insufficiently poetic. And bad poets attract no women.

My *ayeyo* bequeathed me this reverence for language. It was given to her, and she fulfilled her parental duty by making sure I understood my role in upholding the sacred love of language. When I was a very young child, living as a nomad in that distant valley, Ayeyo began encouraging me to memorize poetry and proverbs so that I could begin using more figurative language in my daily conversation. She taught me to use powerful imagery in my speech by memorizing poems, so that it would become second nature when I spoke everyday Somali.

Ayeyo knew that my ability to use poetic words in social situations would determine my place in society, and that when the time came for me to think about marriage, my mastery of poetic diction and proverbs, the way my words danced as they left my mouth, would attract the most suitable women. She understood that as I became more adept at using poetry in everyday conversation, other adults would take note and understand that I was becoming a man, able to take my place in society.

Wordplay was not just idle fun: it produced genuine power and dignity.

Words in the Somali language live inside you like mystical threads, binding you to the past and spinning you out into the future. Somali words are a legacy, the heritage of a people and a nation. When we gather for food, we eat with our poetry while goats and camels and sheep stretch out across the green valley. When we gather for afternoon tea as the sun is dying, we share our meals with poetry. And when the wind carries war over the land, my father and uncles and cousins and all able-bodied men rise up, grab their weapons to fight, and bury the dead with poetry.

I am a citizen of a nation of poets. In Somalia, our names are poems. The earth is a poem. The sun is a poem.

My mother's words to me about that high-school counselor in Somali had rhythm and technique and sealed something in me that I cannot remove.

"Your destiny," she told me, "is a thousand years old. You can shape it, but you cannot alter it."

Even before the words had left her lips, I captured them and made them my own. Her injunction, uttered in lyrical Somali, formed in me a bulwark against that high-school counselor's advice. As I looked at Mama's face, mouth, and lips and listened to her admonition, my brain was spinning. Mama always said the right thing.

"Trust your intuition," she once explained. "Never carry any regrets. Learn from your past, but trust your future."

And: "Smiling is the best form of charity. God always favors the prayers of the weak."

I cherished her advice. Now she was giving me more priceless words.

"It was your departed father's wish," she said, "peace be upon him, that you get a good education. Your father may not be here with us, but his words must live in you. We demand that you get a good college education. You listen to us and to no one else."

I ran into the counselor again later, when he was teaching at the local community college I attended after high school. One day, he walked past me when I was sitting in the cafeteria, holding a cup of coffee. He sat down and pulled out a burlap backpack, took out a homemade sandwich, and started eating. He looked directly at me, but did not speak.

He knew what he had said. If I had taken his advice, I would still be pumping gas. He stared at me.

Was he feeling guilty?

18

I WAS LIVING ON THE COLLEGE CAMPUS, BUT I OFTEN VISITED home so I could help my family. I was sitting with my mother sipping tea and watching television: *Cops* and *America's Most Wanted*. As a practical matter, Mama knew nothing about the American justice system, only what she observed on those programs. But they were Mama's link to America.

As she watched black men flee armed white men in uniforms, only to be locked up and taken away to God knows where, those sights and sounds awakened in her belly dormant memories of militiamen hunting and killing.

She made a vague connection between the police she saw on the television and the militiamen she knew from back home in Somalia, so she was always trying to watch everything and learn more so she could keep tabs on her children and stop them from ending up like the victims she saw on those television programs.

In her anxiety, Mama once sat me down and, looking directly into my eyes, made a vow.

"You are my first son. That means, in the absence of your father, you are now the man in the house. If you go the wrong way and your siblings follow in your footsteps"—she looked at me with serious eyes—"I will never forgive you even in death."

One late summer afternoon the telephone rang.

"Here, you talk to them," Mama said as she handed the phone to me.

"Hello?" I said into the phone.

"May I speak to Hamud's parents?" a stern female voice asked. Hamud was my fourteen-year-old brother, who lived at home with Mama and was just starting high school.

"Yes," I replied. "Speaking." Since my mother did not recognize the English language, I was the one authorized to speak for her.

"I'm sorry to tell you, Hamud has been arrested and is in jail. We can only release him to his parents, so you will have to come down and get him."

"What happened? Why was he arrested?"

"I'm not authorized to say anything to you over the telephone." I could distinguish by this time some differences in the diction of white and black Americans. The woman on the phone sounded like a black woman in a white town. "You're going to need to come down and get him."

"My mother doesn't speak English and is not feeling well. Can you release him to me? I'm his oldest brother. I can drive over there right now."

"Okay," she said. "Come down right away, while I'm still here on duty."

As I put down the phone, my breathing became heavy.

I did not want our mother to know about Hamud's arrest, but there was no way to keep her from finding out.

She had survived when all she knew in Somalia had died. While she was still in her thirties, my father had suffered a slow, agonizing death from untreated lung cancer, leaving her with seven very young children, ages one to thirteen. Rather than seek another marriage, she dedicated her life to feeding and raising us. Then, within a year, civil war broke out in Somalia, and she took us by the hand and fled the war zone.

Walking many miles through dangerous jungle and rebel territory with all of us in tow, she went days without food and water. Whatever little food she came across, she gave to us.

Time and again, what rescued us from death at the hands of the militia was her mastery of everyday language and conversation, the nimbleness and tact with which she manipulated words, and her flair for Somali figures of speech and poetic diction.

And now, here in America, whatever she knew and felt, she had no words to express. Whenever someone spoke English, all Mama could do was open her mouth, stretch her lips apart, and show her fake teeth—she'd lost her front teeth in the war—in a smile.

"So what is it? What's going on?" Mama asked.

I didn't want to say anything, so I fumbled around for a few minutes, putting on my shirt and shoes.

Mama sat motionless, staring at me. "Talk to me. What is it?"

"Nothing, Mama," I said. "It's nothing."

Here, in America, I was her lookout, her ears, her eyes, and I knew she couldn't do anything to help my brother. I could not avoid her gaze.

"What was that all about on the phone? Tell me."

"Hamud has been arrested. But he's being released, and they want me to come down and pick him up." With that, I started to head to my car. Before I could get to the front door, my mother asked me—somewhat casually, as if the news that her son had been arrested had not yet had time to sink in—"But who is this 'they' you keep talking about?"

"The police. But it's okay. I'm going to go down and get him out."

To ease her distress, I maintained a calm facade. Inside I was agitated.

"You hold on and wait a minute, Boyah. You're not going down there without me."

I walked outside to my car. Mama jogged barefoot to keep up with me, carrying her shoes. She jumped into the passenger seat and slipped them on.

This was not going to be easy. We drove to the brick police building where Hamud was being held. I got out first, and waited for Mama.

As we approached the precinct slowly, it occurred to me that we did not even know what the charges were, or how serious Hamud's situation might actually be.

"Are you Hamud's brother?" a light-skinned black woman wearing a police uniform asked as we walked into the station.

"Yes," I replied. "This is our mother."

"All right," she said. "Sign this release, and Hamud is free to go."

"Do you mind telling us what he did?"

"He was arrested joyriding with four other teenagers."

I translated for Mama, who nodded.

The officer continued, "One of the kids stole his father's car, and his father called the police. One of our officers spotted the car, and inside we found stolen videos."

"What happens now?" I asked. Since Hamud was so young, I was hoping this was not going to be a big deal.

It was late summer, and Mama was wearing a long dress

with long sleeves and a headscarf. She was trapped inside her grief and within her native language: there was nothing she could say for herself or her son.

"Just go home for now, and you'll receive a court date by mail."

After a brief wait, two white officers brought Hamud out, releasing him to us.

When I saw him, a red ball of blistering anger lifted from my lower belly, pushing into my throat. I wanted to drag him out to the car, take out my belt, and beat him into submission so that he would never think about making the same mistake again.

Mama remained mute, as if she were stifling her fury.

As we drove home, Hamud appeared defeated. He knew Mama was livid.

"So, Hamud," I said. "Who were these other kids?"

"Just some of my friends."

"The white kids you hang out with?"

"Of course. I don't have that many black friends."

At home, Hamud leaped up the stairs to his room two at a time, and Mama was directly behind him. When he entered his bedroom, Mama kept going right along with him. Then, grabbing a coat hanger, she raised it high and smashed it down, whacking him numerous times.

"Mama, this is America," Hamud begged. "You can't do this, Mama."

Hamud was three years old when we made our escape from Somalia. He never knew our father, and he remembered nothing about the war, nothing about Mama's desperate struggle to protect him, feed his belly, and carry him to freedom and safety in America.

We were now living in the projects, in subsidized housing surrounded by a metal fence, separating us from the white neighbors nearby. On the other side of that fence the houses were bigger and more attractive, the trimmed lawns greener and more enticing, the backyards often equipped with refreshing swimming pools. The white people living on that side rarely, if ever, spoke to the black residents on our side. They never returned our greetings or struck up a conversation.

Coming from Somalia as she did, my mother understood the behavior of the white people on the other side of the fence as a form of tribal distinction, so she really did not care whether they spoke to us or not. Her children had shelter and food and security, and that was all she cared about.

But the idea that Hamud had crossed over to hang out with some white kids and then ended up handcuffed and in jail—that was something Mama could not accept.

Hamud, on the other hand, came to America so young that he could hardly be considered Somali, much less a pastoral nomad like me. He was attracted by that white world and its aloofness, and his sense of self-worth had become jumbled and distorted.

"You're not one of those white boys," she howled. "Do you understand that?" In her mind, a good whipping with a hanger was better than being taken in by the police and possibly executed. Hamud could only take the beating.

I ran upstairs, calling out, "Mama, hold on, just calm down now, please." Grabbing her hand and attempting to take the hanger from her, I tried to stop her. "Mama, control yourself."

After a few moments, she relented.

"I just don't want to see him hanging around with those good-for-nothing white boys in the neighborhood." She pointed at Hamud. "How can he do this and disobey me after all we've been through?"

Mama and I went back down into the living room. I took a seat and turned on the television again. Mama poured a cup of water and gulped it down.

She filled it up again and brought it over to me. I gulped water too. Suddenly she stood up in prayer. She prayed a little longer and louder than usual.

Afterward, she sat next to me in front of the television. "You need to spend more time with Hamud. Take him out with you when you go."

"Huh?" I said, perplexed. I wasn't sure how I was going to do that because Hamud was quite a bit younger than I was. But I had to do what she told me. "Sure."

"He's too young to be out there on his own. Look at that, he wasn't even driving when the police just grabbed him and locked him up. And now all those white kids over there are going to be out looking for him."

"I got it," I said. "Hamud is stupid."

"He needs to be with his own, someone who will watch out for him." She paused. "I want you to step up and keep an eye on him."

On the television, *Cops* was still playing.

19

MY COLLEGE CLASS SCHEDULE ENDED ON THURSDAY, SO I RE- turned home and found myself driving through town with Hamud in tow, as Mama wished.

Dressed up, hip-hop fashion, I was wearing my cologne and sporting a large Afro. I had a girlfriend and carried a Nokia flip phone. I had upgraded my ride to an old used luxury car. I had a large CD collection. I thought I knew a thing or two about life in America.

I told Hamud to reach over and shove in a gangsta rap CD. There we were, driving through town with the windows rolled down and the music blaring. If you asked me where we were heading, I could not have told you. We were on the road to nowhere and everywhere.

In my peripheral vision, I spotted a state trooper approach and drive by in the opposite direction.

"Did you notice that police car?" I asked Hamud.

"Yeah," he said, gesturing toward the cruiser.

"I bet he's going to turn around and stop us. Listen, I need you to buckle up."

I grabbed my seat belt and fastened it and made sure my brother did the same. And then, in my rearview mirror, I watched as that police cruiser made a U-turn and started following us.

"See. I told you."

"What?" my brother said, panicking.

"He turned around. Now he's following us."

"No way!" He turned his head to look back. "Damn! You're right. There he is, driving up right behind us."

"He's gonna stop us, but listen, don't say a word. Let me do the talking."

They are afraid, I know that. The white people and their police force are afraid. What frightens them is not the thirteen percent of the population, the black people, that they fixate on. What frightens them, in the end, is the memory of their own ruthless brutality, the judgment of their own conscience. The past always comes alive in the present, and with the passage of time the history of race takes its shape in each individual soul, black and white.

Sure enough, the trooper pulled us over. I turned down the music and handed him my license and registration as usual. Neither Hamud nor I reacted. We sat silently and obeyed.

He walked back to his cruiser and returned after a few minutes.

"You're all set."

He gave no hint as to why he'd stopped us. We certainly did not ask.

I took off and right away headed for the highway, seeking freedom and release. The only thing I knew to do was to get on the highway and drive, with my music blaring, those voices crying out for justice. As I grew older, I gained a deeper appreciation of music, and my taste became much broader—Bob Dylan, Cat Stevens, Frank Sinatra, John Lennon, Harry Belafonte, and Ben E. King. I ventured beyond rap into a wider world of musical expression and found there a place for myself, adding new tones and modes, a new musical vocabulary for my griefs and joys. The sensation produced by music has always touched my soul and soothed my temper—without ever breaking the grip of my frustration. Harassment made me restless.

Like a shark lurking beneath the surface, what lay ahead I couldn't see.

"Hamud, pull out a CD," I said. "Put something on."

He put in N.W.A.'s *Straight Outta Compton* and "Fuck tha Police."

I always liked that song. The beat was intense; the lyrics spoke to my mood.

I identified with the anger, the sense of truth being shouted directly to white people. I was hearing a report about what life was like to have a black body in a world run by people who thought they were white. "Fuck tha Police" wasn't a cute slogan or a marketing strategy. It was a genuine philosophical and ethical position that put in my mouth the words that were just a feeling in my heart, that red ball of fury, inchoate and amorphous.

Now it had a voice and a shape. The song was the form of my resistance. Decades before George Floyd was executed, N.W.A. spoke for George Floyd.

N.W.A. are bards of the black worldview. No doubt about it.

Now something was emerging in my spirit, an intuition about what was happening.

I pictured Mama carrying Hamud on one hip, trudging along with bullets ricocheting nearby and bombs exploding in the distance. On her other hip, she is lugging rice and corn, plates and pots, and all her children are following behind. She feeds us; and the little bit of grain and rice she has left over she sells to militiamen with demons in their eyes who might just as easily take the grain and take her life.

I see her withering away, like a lone tree without rain.

I was beginning to feel like there was something in all that which I needed to respect and honor, something I needed to see more clearly. I was the eldest, certainly, the role model. Yet here I was sitting in the car with my fourteen-year-old brother Hamud, cursing and railing against the police. After a couple of minutes, I turned and pressed eject. Then I grabbed the CD and tossed it out the window.

"What are you doing?" Hamud exclaimed, his mouth open in shock.

"Never mind. Go ahead, put in another CD."

Hamud put in Tupac Shakur's *Me Against the World*. "Dear Mama" started to play. For a while our heads moved back and forth to the rhythm of the beat.

Hamud was too young to know Mama the way I knew her. As I drove along that late-summer afternoon, both of us rocking our heads, I recalled how, to protect us, Mama often told us not to trust what she did not approve of—and she did not approve of men wearing jewelry, any kind of necklaces or bracelets or earrings.

Whenever I came back to the house and parked my car, I always took off the hip-hop-inspired jewelry I wore to show off to my friends and stashed it beneath the car seat before I went in. Once inside and at home with my mother, I concentrated on my studies and stood on the prayer mat so she could see her son praying to Almighty God.

Whenever I spoke Somali in her presence, I did my utmost to impress her by mixing in a lot of metaphors and proverbs so she would think proudly of me as a real Somali man, my father's son. At home with her, I always wrapped myself in a Somali sarong and listened only to Somali music. I ate the rice and chicken and goat meat my mother prepared, but I was always thinking about hamburgers, hot dogs, potato chips, macaroni and cheese, and meat loaf.

I was hardly out of the house again and back into my car before I would grab my red hat and retrieve my silver chain from beneath the car seat and put on Tupac, Dr. Dre, Snoop Dogg, and Biggie Smalls. All the music I liked.

When "Dear Mama" finished, I pressed eject. The CD came out, and I grabbed it and tossed it out the open window.

"What's gotten into you!" Hamud screamed. "Are you nuts or something?" He shoved my shoulder in irritation. He was staring at me with his eyes fixed, trying to figure out if I had gone mad.

But I was fine, and Hamud would be okay. We were good kids living in a mad white country.

I pushed back. "I'm letting it all go, trying to show you something!"

"What are you talking about?" His mouth was agape, his head turned to look back at the highway behind. "Are you all right?"

"I'm okay. Put in another one."

"Why?" he exploded. "Just so you can throw it out the window again?"

"No, not really." I shook my head. I turned my eyes from the empty highway to meet his gaze and told him, "Go ahead. Put in one of your favorite CDs."

He flipped through the albums, popped in Dead Prez's *Let's Get Free*, and played "They School."

As the words railed against an education as the embodiment of white oppression and values, I was listening and thinking.

In Africa, Mama and my father always put education first, so in America, Mama expected Hamud to go to school and then come home and study and pray. But Hamud wanted something else: he wanted escape from all that, from the aggravation of school and Mama.

Her preaching. Her beating. Her yelling. Her food. Her prayers. Her silent tears streaming down her face.

What was his alternative?

To live free like white Americans in white America.

As that song blasted from the speakers, I was thinking. What was the real alternative? What were Hamud and I becoming in America?

Driving free on the highway, we had no idea what was coming down the road. We did not know—or rather, we chose not to know—that in the real white America awaiting us, black people were not free and never had been.

The dead do not lie—you can ask Michael Brown, Ahmaud Arbery, George Floyd, and Breonna Taylor. Their corpses tell the story.

My mother knew something about murder and chaos and the fragility of life in a foreign land. She knew something about surviving corruption and decay and the savagery that never dies. She knew something about living with the distortion of despair and hopelessness in a land where the trust that binds people in society is shattered like a glass thrown against a wall.

I had seen all this before when warlords in my childhood Somalia used words not to kill but to inspire others to kill, to stir up and agitate those stricken with poverty and ignorance, looking for an escape from their plight. The more I tolerated and internalized the continuous harassment and threats, the more I belonged to America.

I was leading a double life and fighting against my own mother. It was a classic case of double consciousness. In my confusion, I was dancing between two worlds, and now my younger brother was starting to get into trouble.

At that, I had no choice but to take decisive action.

Sam Cooke singing "A Change Is Gonna Come" represented everything I valued.

Such was my aspiration for Hamud—for him to give up his troublemaking friends and develop more positive relationships, to begin to see beyond one kind of music, one kind of friend.

With Hamud staring in shock, I again pressed eject and tossed Dead Prez out the window. Like a machine, I jettisoned all my CDs onto the blacktop of the rolling highway.

Done.

20

A KNOCK ON MAMA'S DOOR.

"Who's that?" Mama asked me. "Go and find out."

Rising to my feet, I went to the door. "Who's there?"

"Hello?"

The voice was a black woman's, so I opened the door.

"Oh!" I said, suddenly recognizing her. It was the female black cop who had called us about getting Hamud released.

"May I come in?" she asked, her soft eyes holding mine like a warm hand.

"Please, come in," I said politely.

"Where's your mother?" she asked. As I was opening the door, Mama had walked upstairs to the bathroom to fix herself up.

"Mama!" I called out, then turned back to our visitor. "She'll be right down. Have a seat."

"Do you mind if we sit outside?" the woman asked. "It's nice out." When she came to the door, she must have seen the chairs sitting outside in the yard.

"Sure," I replied. "We can go sit down, and Mama will join us in a minute."

This woman police officer was average height, with light

skin and brown curly hair. She was wearing a short-sleeved black dress, and I could see that she was rather buff, her arms and legs muscular. She stepped off the porch, and I followed her around to the side of the house near the fence, where we sat down.

After a moment, Mama walked out of the house and joined us. "Hi," she said, with her usual and prolonged display of teeth.

Then she turned to look at me, as if asking me to translate. I could tell from her expression that she recognized the policewoman.

"Hello," the cop responded. "I'm Officer Roshani, but you can just call me Roshani." She paused. "Do you remember me?"

"Mama," I said. "You remember Roshani, don't you?"

"Of course I do," she replied, stretching her lips in a smile. "Welcome to our home," she offered in heavily accented, broken English.

I conveyed Mama's appreciation to Roshani.

Mama excused herself, returned to the house, and came back a few moments later carrying bottles of water, a thermos of tea, sugar in a dish, and three ceramic cups. She laid out everything on the table. Mama always gave food to people who visited our house.

"Tell her to take some tea and water," she asked me to translate. I did as she asked.

"Thank you," Roshani responded. "That's nice of you."

Roshani was comfortable and friendly and conveyed none of the tough demeanor we associated with the police. She seemed more like one of us.

"Go ahead, drink." Mama extended her hand to offer Roshani a bottle of water.

"Your son is in real trouble," Roshani began. "He's facing jail time."

"But he's only fourteen, and this is his first time arrested!" I said. "Besides, he didn't steal anything. That was those white boys he was with who took the car and the videos."

"Well," she said, shaking her head, "I understand what you're saying, but you may not understand completely how things work here in America."

Although the sky was clear, tiny raindrops were misting the air. In Somalia, rain is always a sign of God's blessing, so my mother was thinking Roshani's visit was a good sign.

"He's really not a bad kid," I insisted. "I know he made a mistake, but we can work with him and help him."

"You have to understand," she replied with a bit of hesitation in her voice, as if she were telling us something intimate and private that only family members would share with one another. "Of the four suspects, your brother was the only one who was black."

"Yeah, I know," I said.

"Moreover, the other three kids arrested with him have all had run-ins with the law," she continued, pointing to the reality facing Hamud. "And the kid who was driving and stole his father's car is on probation."

"I understand." My eyes alternated between Mama and Roshani.

As Roshani spoke, I listened and translated everything for Mama. She was watching Roshani and trying to follow each of her words so that not one would escape her. All the while, she was cracking her knuckles, wiping her face with her hand, and playing with her lower lip. She was clearly getting more and more agitated.

"So," I asked, "is the white kid going to jail who stole the car and was driving? Is he getting time?"

"No," Roshani said. "Even though he was on probation at the time, he's not going to jail. He might go to a juvenile detention center for a while, but he won't have to go to jail."

My head was exploding. "But Hamud will?"

"Unfortunately, yes." She turned to look at Mama. "Make sure your mother understands what I'm saying. Tell her what I just said."

"I did," I said to Roshani. "What can we do? Will you be able to help?"

"I think so. That's why I'm coming to you here without my police uniform."

"Thank you. We appreciate what you're doing. It's hard to figure out what's going on."

"Certainly," she said in a small, timid voice. "Maybe you might think about sending Hamud back to Egypt, getting him out of this environment. Don't you have family there?"

Mama nodded, as if she understood something about Egypt.

"Egypt!" I exclaimed. "Why Egypt?"

"Aren't you from there?" she asked, holding her bottle of half-sipped water.

"No, not at all," I said. "We're from Somalia—you know, East Africa."

"Right. I'm sorry," she said. "In any case, it's better to send him away before he becomes institutionalized."

I repeated the word *institutionalized* over and over in my mind and then practiced it with my tongue a few times so I could remember to look it up later on. Because I really did not understand the word, I did not want to waste it.

"Maybe that would be a good idea," I said, my eyes traveling between her and Mama.

"You're lucky you can send him somewhere else and get him away from here," she added. "I wish I had a country I could go to and get away from things."

That was the real white America I heard in her voice and saw in her posture: there was no possibility of escape. Roshani was trapped in a place where she felt rejected.

If America rejected this beautiful Roshani, whose family had been here for four hundred years, would it ever accept Mama, Hamud, or me?

"So," I offered. "We can try that. If you can help us manage to keep Hamud out of jail, we can arrange to send him back home to Somalia."

The irony was that Hamud would be safer with Ayeyo in the Nugaal Valley in Somalia than on the streets of America. US democracy was more threatening to black skin than Somalia. Ayeyo could help Hamud pull himself together.

"He'll definitely be better off there with less craziness to distract him," I said. "We really appreciate your help getting him through this."

"Unfortunately," Roshani continued, "I'm not assigned to his case, but I'm going to be getting in touch with the officer in charge and following how the case is handled. I'll make sure that he appears before a judge who will be more sympathetic."

Policing while black is not easy, but Roshani's conscience was more exacting than her uniform. The blue uniform took George Floyd's life and Michael Brown's life and Breonna Taylor's life; so even though Roshani did not know us, she recognized that we were weak and unprotected and that nobody wanted us.

We had nowhere else to go, nowhere else to hide, no way to seek justice. And that was enough for her to take us into her confidence.

Something beyond her uniform was more insistent in her consciousness and more exacting: you are American, and you wear the uniform, but the law you serve does not always protect. As you realize that, what do you do? If survival is your life goal, you go along and keep your mouth shut: you keep your job, but defy your conscience.

If you refuse to go along, your job is on the line.

So you end up double-minded: smiling and cheerful, but determined to make what is broken in the system work for everyone. Your only choice is revolution without the bloodshed.

That is how you survive in white America.

Roshani understood that standing up for us was protecting her own soul.

"Oh, thank you for your help with the judge," I said. "That would be great."

"But I warn you, it will take time to get a court date, and you'll have to find a lawyer."

"Thank you," Mama said, interrupting out of gratitude. "Thank you."

"While he's waiting for that court date, he absolutely cannot get into any more trouble. Because if he does, they're going to throw the book at him, and he'll end up right back in jail."

"I understand," I said. "We'll watch him."

"You know, justice here doesn't work the same for everyone. The way things are set up, the system often plays favorites. It sticks up for the white kids and then blames the black kids and throws them under the bus. I don't want that to happen to Hamud."

"That's all very sad," I said.

"I would hate to see Hamud go to jail, while his white friends with criminal records are only sent to juvenile detention. Tell your mother." Roshani stood up and took a sip of her tea. "So you're going to get a letter with a court date. I'm going to be looking out in the meantime to see that he gets a fair trial this time around."

"We truly appreciate everything you're doing," I said in a humbled voice. "Thank you so very much."

"But remember, tell her, Hamud can't get into any more trouble. And he needs to stop hanging out with those white friends of his over there in the neighborhood."

"We'll talk to him and make sure."

Mama was listening and smiling, her only way to communicate what she was feeling.

At that moment, Hamud stepped out of the house and joined us. He was smiling because he didn't understand how much trouble he was in.

"Hi there," Roshani said. "Come over here for a minute, let's talk. You know, you're facing jail time? Do you realize that?"

"But I didn't do anything," he protested. "My friends came to pick me up, that was it."

"You really don't get it, do you?" she scolded him.

"But I didn't steal anything."

"But you were the only black kid in the group, right?" she said. "Is that correct?"

"Yes."

"So you're the only one who's going to be facing jail time."

"Even if I didn't do anything?"

"Yes, even if you didn't do anything," she repeated. "The fact that you were in the vehicle and that you're black is enough around here for you to do time in jail."

"That's really sad," I interjected.

"It's sad, but that's the situation." She sipped tea and cleared her throat. "I'm sorry, but there is one kind of justice for whites and another for blacks."

Her stark declaration was chilling. Roshani felt our hurt, and we felt she was akin to us.

Mama used to drill into us endlessly that we were under an obligation to aid everyone who needed our help. This became her mantra, particularly during our escape from the war, because so many people had stepped in and risked their own lives to help us survive; in fact, the only reason we were able to survive was because, at critical moments, someone had helped us.

Now, here in America, Roshani had once again saved us from catastrophe, and it seemed her African bloodline had carried her to us for just this purpose. She was Mama's metaphorical African daughter. We were her lost family.

Roshani, Mama, Hamud, and I sat in those chairs, looking at one another, for a while.

"Tell her," Mama said as she turned her head to me, "I'd like to give her a hug."

"Mama wants to hug you," I said, translating Mama's message to Roshani.

"Of course," Roshani said.

They embraced.

"Now, I've got to go."

I watched Roshani and Mama hug. Mama was tearing up. The clouds in the far distance held rain, but where we were was still clear and sunny, with a gentle breeze.

We all stood up and walked a few steps behind Roshani as she walked back to her white Ford Explorer, opened the door, got in, turned on the engine, and looked back to wave at us.

We waved back at her with all our mouths open.

"Bye," Mama said, and Roshani drove off.

That was the last we ever saw of her.

Mama turned around and took a few steps back into the house, and Hamud and I followed. She held the door open for us and, standing in the kitchen, stared steadily at Hamud. Her lips were quivering, and she was rubbing her hands together as if thinking.

In this painfully beautiful land, she had no words to help her child Hamud. I too was thinking, but not intensely like Mama. Walking past her, I went to the living room, grabbed the remote control, and sat down on the sofa. Mama and Hamud and I sat in silence.

To take my mind off Hamud, I started flipping channels. We skipped *Cops* and began to watch a documentary on the Discovery Channel about Mongolia and its rugged nomadic tribes.

They were on the move. They had horses for travel, yaks and camels with two humps for meat and milk, and eagles trained for hunting.

Their land was vast and rough, and they lived on the edge of survival. Their lives were bound to that particular tract of land, like other nomads, and it was there that they lived and moved about in freedom, protecting their herds and raising their families, worshipping their God and enjoying their culture.

As I watched, the landscape changed from mountains and hills to sand and desert, from snowdrifts to dry heat. Then I saw a naked African woman carrying a child bound at her waist and sucking at her sagging breast, a basket filled with wild fruit balanced on her head. At a pool of water, she bent down and filled her water jug made from animal hide.

Then she journeyed home, dropped her water jug and basket, and unwrapped the child gently. Soon her naked husband appeared, coming home from the hunt, carting a wild pig impaled on a pole. My mother was watching in fascination. Although she had grown up living the nomadic life with my *ayeyo* in a valley with goats, camels, and sheep, she had never before seen naked Africans.

Here in America, we were seeing ourselves on television in an entirely different light—naked and wild and barbaric. In Africa, we used to watch black Americans in movies and wonder how they could be so lazy and drug-addicted and ungrateful for the opportunity of living in America. Those images led us to think ourselves superior to those black Americans we saw in the movies: given the chance to live in America, we would certainly do better and succeed.

Such was our thinking in the refugee camp when we made friends with the family living in the white tent across from ours, a mother and father, two girls, and two preteen boys. When our two families saw our names listed at the camp's information tent and realized we were going to America, the joy inside did weird things to us. We could not sleep. We could not eat. We could not even count the days or hours or minutes—we counted the seconds until we could leave for America—that star, that heaven on earth.

Our families received resettlement green cards on the same day. We came to New York City on the same flight. We had no inkling what lay ahead, but that family discovered too late that the movie image of black Americans applied to them as well.

One son was turned on to drugs. Humiliated by his addiction, he committed suicide. The second son ran into trouble with the police and wound up with a long prison term. When the parents disapproved of their daughter's boyfriend, she eloped and disappeared. The father succumbed to a heart attack. One by one, America took all of them.

They survived war and death in Africa, but America broke them and carried them off. America is democratic: every black person is, in the end, simply another black body.

After some months, we went with Hamud to face the judge. Roshani's plan for us prevailed. Hamud received eight weeks of community service. My mother was afraid that he would repeat his stupidity and end up in jail again, so she took Roshani's advice and sent him back to Somalia to live in the Nugaal Valley with our *ayeyo*.

Something in me wished I were going back too. But my life was too rooted in America now.

Mama was relieved when Hamud left, because she had nightmares of him being raped in prison. "I would rather he be killed in Somalia than raped in an American jail," she said. "There in Somalia, he'll either be killed or straighten himself out. But he will not be raped."

I was never able to find out just what happened to Roshani. Even if we never find her or see her again, however, we honor her in her absence the way we Somalis honor our own. We speak her name during our afternoon tea. We recall her in the poetry we use in conversation. We honor her in our silent prayers.

We honor her by giving a helping hand to others in her name.

21

SOMETIME AFTER MAMA SENT HAMUD BACK TO SOMALIA, SHE
and I were again sitting on chairs under the trees near the fence
outside. Bahdoon, my thirteen-year-old brother, a year younger
than Hamud, was upstairs in his room playing the video games
that obsessed him. My younger sisters were staring into the
TV, studying Tom and Jerry cartoons. My older sister was up
in her room with her husband, tending to their child.

It was late afternoon. We were having tea when a white uniformed cop holding a mug shot approached us. We thought he
had the wrong house.

"What does he want?" Mama asked me. "Talk to him."

"Do you know this guy? Have you seen him around here?"
the cop growled at us, holding out the mug shot. It was Hamud.

He handed the picture to me. I passed it to Mama. We looked
at it together.

"What does he want with Hamud?" Mama asked.

"I'm not sure," I replied. "Let me ask."

But as soon as I turned to the cop, he talked over me. "I'm
looking for this guy Hamud in the picture. He crashed into a
parked car and fled the scene."

"What?" I asked. "Hamud is in Africa."

He looked angry. "Where?"

"Hamud is in Africa," Mama said in Somali. "Tell him what I said."

She opened her mouth with frequent smiles as her way to communicate politely with this cop standing over us and talking. But he was not returning her smiles.

Mama did not speak English, and my father was dead. I was Mama's mouth, eyes, and ears. I was everything to her. I did not trust that cop. I did not care if he was wearing a uniform or not.

"My brother Hamud is in Africa," I said calmly. "He's not your guy."

"When did he go to Africa?"

"Hamud has been in Africa for some time."

I was certain he could pick up some of the annoyance in my words. He could see the aggravation on my face. "When did this hit-and-run you're talking about take place?" I asked.

"Today," he said. "Just a few hours ago."

Mama was sitting there, speechless, her face blank.

"Hamud," she said finally. She spoke English in her own way. "Africa."

The cop was becoming increasingly agitated and loud, and he quickly escalated the situation. "The guy in this mug shot did a hit-and-run this afternoon, and I'm told he lives here," he insisted. "Now where the hell is he?"

Hamud was not even old enough to have a license. Once again, I was beginning to think that living black in America was beyond preposterous. I had not survived war and refugee camps only to lie down and accept subjugation. There is a God overlooking everything below, including this white two-legged creature of my species who was causing me trouble.

I refused to be humiliated; humiliation frightened me more than anything else. "I'd rather die like a man than live like a coward," as Tupac sang.

When you are harassed repeatedly and the harassment turns into humiliation, you feel overwhelmed, and despair takes over. Then you get upset and react.

That's when you lose, and then your body belongs to them. They got you. They can put you in jail. They can even murder you. When you react in despair, your body becomes theirs—which is why they try to get you upset in the first place.

Harassed and tormented for over four hundred years, black people cried and begged, marched and prayed, danced and sang. Such practices are nothing more than a cry of the heart: "Let me live."

Just as we were trying to explain to this cop that Hamud was nowhere around, Bahdoon happened to step out of the house. As soon as the officer laid eyes on him, the cop immediately, and without any warning, confronted Bahdoon and reached for his handcuffs.

"Okay, guy. You're coming with me."

"No, he is not!" I yelled out. "You've got the wrong guy! He is not your suspect!"

"That's okay. He's coming with me anyway. And we can sort it all out down at the station."

His mind was made up. If he could not find Hamud, he was going to arrest anyone who came along—anybody, no matter who. So now he wanted to arrest Bahdoon, and they could celebrate the capture of another runaway slave down at the police station.

I was livid.

Mama jumped up and grabbed Bahdoon's arm, all the while

yelling at me in Somali: "Tell him he's got the wrong boy!" She thrust her body between Bahdoon and the cop while I locked arms with her to block him from reaching Bahdoon.

"It's not going to happen," I said angrily. "We don't trust you."

"Trust's got nothing to do with it," he said. "Go get your brother, or I'm taking this one in."

"What?" I reacted. "Maybe you can just pull out your gun and shoot me on the spot before you humiliate me." I totally lost it. "I will only die once, and I'm certainly not afraid of you. You're a racist cop, and I'm going to call my attorney right now!"

I did not have an attorney. The idea came to my mind because I'd picked up from television that the police were afraid of attorneys. Lawyers, I read, run America.

The policeman froze and stood back, looking at us with the picture in his hand.

His posture softened, and his eyes lost their intensity.

He put away the handcuffs and dropped his hands to his side. His chin turned toward the sky, as if he were thinking. Then, without a word, he just turned around and left, carrying Hamud's mug shot with him.

"Any nigga that survives *this* nightmare is my goddamn hero," Dave Chappelle once remarked.

22

ONE DAY IN THE WINTER OF MY SENIOR YEAR OF COLLEGE, I left the campus library and stepped outside. Walking on the packed snow, I stretched my back, craned my neck to the left and right, and cracked my knuckles.

The sky was gray, but random clouds were visible far off in the distance. It was Friday afternoon, and I was happy because Friday night was my favorite time of the week. I had just traded in my Chevy for a Honda and wanted to enjoy it a little bit.

My head waltzed in the gray clouds.

My heart was beating way ahead of me as I thought about getting together with my friends that night. Sporting a well-trimmed goatee and a bald-fade hairstyle, at that age I appreciated my own pretty-boy good looks. But before I could go out, Mama had asked me to go pick up an elderly Somali man who lived twenty miles away and help him do his shopping errands.

I walked around to the back of the library where my car was parked, got in, turned on the engine, adjusted my red hat backward, and rolled the windows down. I had begun to collect CDs again, but I hid them from my brothers because they were too young and I wanted to protect their minds. But I still loved listening to that music, so I popped Tupac Shakur into the CD player, playing "To Live & Die in L.A." I reclined my seat a bit, cranked up the volume, and took off, bobbing my head to the beat. I let the song shower my soul. My car was on the move, my head was rocking, the air was slipping through the slightly ajar windows, and Tupac's rap was blazing out. Driving down the highway, I felt free and powerful—as if I could fly and touch the moon and the stars.

I picked up the elderly gentleman at his home, and we headed to the local pharmacy to drop off his prescription. We pulled in to the parking lot, and I parked in the fire lane in front of the pharmacy and left the old man sitting in the passenger seat while I ran in, with the car heater still running because it was the dead of winter and freezing.

The ground was wet. The sky was pregnant with snow. I needed only a minute to go in. I returned to my car and to the old man waiting for me in fewer than ten minutes, only to discover a uniformed policeman walking around and inspecting my car.

"I am so sorry, Officer," I said to the policeman writing down my license-plate number. "Please don't write me a ticket. I'm leaving right now."

I jumped into the car, but he came around to my driver's side and glanced at the back of the car, where books, papers and my backpack were scattered about in the back seat.

"So, are you a student around here?" he asked as he nodded toward my things.

"Yes," I answered. "I am so sorry."

"Shut the engine off. Get out of the car!"

The old man sat next to me, confused and clueless: he was looking around, asking me what the cop wanted, but I was laser-focused on the cop and what he was saying.

I did as I was told and stood beside the car as the policeman examined my license.

"Where are you from?" he said, squinting. Listening to my accent, he could tell I was not a native-born American.

"I'm from Africa."

"Where in Africa?"

"Somalia."

He nodded, but his eyes darkened with suspicion. "Okay," he said angrily. "I'm going to need to search you."

After some years of schooling, my English was considerably improved, shaped by the culture of hip-hop and the language of fashion, art, and style. I took off my red hat.

"What?" I said, taken off guard by his hostility. "Sir, am I under arrest?"

"Not yet. I need to make sure you don't have any weapons on you."

"I know I parked in the fire lane, but I'll move now," I said apologetically. Mama had warned all of us in the family always to obey people in uniform and apologize whenever they stopped us—*when*, she emphasized, not *if*.

After so many apologies had spilled from my lips, the man in the uniform seemed to soften a bit. None of that, however, deterred him from shoving me up against my car to search me. I couldn't fathom going to jail. I had not fled civil war in Somalia only to wind up in an American jail. As much as the old man sitting in the car felt a stranger in a foreign land, I felt at home. Not only was I a naturalized American citizen, but everything about me was becoming an American. The Philly cheesesteak I often ate, the Beastie Boys songs I played in the car with the windows halfway rolled down, the Tupac chain that hung from my neck, the everyday English words that often came out of my mouth when I flirted with girls. I was living a contradiction, but I was in love with the fantasy of America.

America was like a dream resurrected from my buried childhood.

My hat cocked to the side, driving with my seat pulled back, my head bobbing to the music, my right hand resting on the wheel and my eyes scanning the road ahead, I had been playing a part in America. Now I found myself again in serious jeopardy.

The old man, still in the car, looked as frightened as a deer in the company of a lion. Standing there confronting the police officer, I just could not imagine getting arrested. The police officer, holding his ticket book, was standing behind me.

I felt my heart pounding under my shirt—I had no idea what to do. I was so skinny that that cop surely knew I posed no threat to him.

"Turn around and put your hands on the hood," he said.

I did as he asked.

I felt his hands pat down my waist and legs and go through my hair. My world was ending. Once this cop arrested me, I, the first son in my family, was going to become a criminal. I was in despair.

"You're suspected of creating a disturbance at the bank over there, and your car matches the description of the suspect's vehicle."

"What bank? What disturbance are you talking about?"

Frantic, I peered over my shoulder at him. For a moment, he seemed surprised that I did not submit passively, and seemed unsure how to proceed.

"Sir, I just pulled up here with this gentleman only ten minutes ago, so I could not have robbed any bank."

Obviously convinced he had his man, the officer did not

even bother to reply. My car was still parked in the fire lane, and the old man was sitting in the passenger seat.

"Before you arrest me, take me to the bank, so you can ask them to identify me."

As a student of America, I had absorbed enough to understand that I had to protect myself. The officer could see that the old man sitting in the car was oblivious and unaware. But to him that was irrelevant. I was nothing but another dangerous black body.

Although he was in the wrong, I remained calm and polite as a first defense strategy, so as not to give him an excuse to harm me. I paused and imagined him pulling out his handcuffs and locking them on me. I was in a humiliating position, and I could see white people walking in and out of the stores, glancing at us furtively.

"Look at the old man sitting in the car," I said. "He doesn't even speak English." But however much I pleaded and apologized, the officer chose to remain silent.

"Sir. Please don't arrest me. I'm not the guy you're looking for."

The cop laughed. "Oh, no. You've been identified. You're the guy. Your car matches the description given to us."

"But it's not me. You have the wrong guy. I'm completely innocent."

Somehow, he was softening. He was not as intense as before. I had a feeling he might now be willing to hear me out a bit.

"Before you arrest me, please take me to the bank and see if they can identify me. You'll see I'm not the person you're looking for."

I was a man with multiple identities, containing multitudes, like Walt Whitman. I was a black man. I was an African. I was African American.

As I stood there in the snow with my head bowed like a wounded bird, I could only keep thinking, Fuck this. Fuck this cop. Fuck it all.

Through the side window of the car, the old man was watching, but there was nothing he could do. Like me, he had no country. The country we knew was no more. The memory of our birth country was nothing but dust.

How many of my childhood friends were now living in the land of the dead? At my worst moments during the war, I used to call on the angel of death. In my imagination, I would ask him to take my soul up and through the clouds and bury my body in a shallow grave so the ants in the soil or the night animals could find me and feast in a frenzy. It was my father's last will and testament that I live free and die with dignity. And now I was engaged in protecting my life from the very country that had revived my hopes for living. I considered telling this white man something of all that, but racing emotions and the fear of going to jail outran every other consideration.

"Let's go," the officer commanded. "To the bank." The urgency of my contrition seemed to have worn down his white-hot hostility.

I walked ahead, and he followed.

Somewhere in me was happy that I was not in handcuffs and that the old man's eyes could follow us, recording the events without words. Beads of sweat began to dampen my butt cheeks. As we approached the bank, he directed me toward the door.

"Right here. Go on in."

He motioned for me to go in first, and he walked in behind me. I felt even more sweat dampen my stomach and armpits.

The scalp of my head began to itch. There were no customers in the bank when we entered, and I was happy about that.

Humiliation and betrayal hovered over me like a covering of snow.

"Is this the one who tore up the place?" he asked an Indian lady standing behind the teller's window.

At first she looked at me without saying anything or making a sound. I returned her stare with silence of my own. One word from her mouth, and I was going to jail.

"Yes." She broke her silence. "That's him."

My heart suddenly dropped, and my head started spinning. A ball of fury rising up from my stomach made it difficult for me to breathe, and my throat itched. My stomach growled and gurgled as my intestines quarreled. Somewhere deep in my rectum hurt. Danger and betrayal were lurking in me and around me.

Here I was about to be falsely arrested and thrown in jail. This is utterly preposterous, I thought.

Preposterous was one of the first words of the English language I fell in love with. Something about that word belonged to me.

The dream I brought to America was preposterous. The scourge of war and the sight of corpses were preposterous. But more preposterous than all else was the America that treated every black man living on its soil as interchangeable and expendable.

I lost my cool. "Think about what you're saying before you speak!" I yelled. "I'm not your suspect. I've never seen you before in my life!"

Then a white woman in her forties came out of the back office and stationed herself beside the Indian woman behind the glass window of the teller's counter.

She focused on me, staring.

"How could I tear up everything," I said, "when I haven't been anywhere near here?"

True, I may have been an American-in-the-making, but I was also my father's first son: going down innocent without a fight was not an option. In an instant, my mind switched into war mode.

"You can't just point a finger at me and say I'm the guy!" I spat the words out. "You've got the wrong guy. You've never seen me before!"

The spinning fan above seemed to stop, as a deafening silence surrounded me.

For a moment, the cop, who was standing behind, did not say anything.

Words choked me, and the Indian woman who identified me as the suspect did not say a word. We were staring at each other, and I was watching the policeman's hand as it rested on his silver handcuffs. I am actually going to prison, I thought.

As my thoughts and emotions collided, the white worker standing behind the glass window was still looking at me closely, as if she were beginning to doubt her colleague.

"No, I'm sorry," the white woman said finally. "That's not him."

A whispered *whoosh* came out of my mouth, and something lifted off my shoulders. I took a deep breath, heavy and hard and loud, as my eyes switched between the cop and the two women behind the glass window.

She continued, "You've got the wrong person."

With a feeling of vindication, I turned to the cop and asked, "Am I free to go now?"

He stepped aside as I turned around, grabbed the door, and

walked out. But then he followed me outside to my car. As I extended my hand to open the car door, I could feel his shadow considering the moment and watching me and thinking about what to make of the situation. It was at just such a moment, as he was getting into his car with the police shadowing him, that Jacob Blake was shot in the back seven times and paralyzed, his three young sons, like this elderly Somali man, helpless witnesses.

Opening the door, I climbed into the driver's seat and turned to look at the old man. He was still sitting there, transfixed, too stunned and terrified to get out and stretch while he waited. He was old. He was an immigrant. He spoke no English.

I smiled with relief and with grief, and he returned the smile.

For a moment, it occurred to me to express relief out loud, but instead somehow wrath and indignation rose up in me instead. At all of them—the cop, that teller, and the bank manager—all of them. I hated them for turning my Friday-afternoon joy into a nightmare of wounded dignity.

Still, the cop was standing there next to my car.

I turned to him. "Is there something else you want from me? I'm good. I'm clear. No longer a suspect. Now please leave me alone."

"Do you have a brother?" he asked, to my surprise.

My innocence had robbed him of his self-confidence. His aggression, having run its course for over four hundred years, needed to be justified, his conscience made clear. The alternative was too awful for him to imagine.

"Yes, I have a brother," I replied. "And so what?"

"Was he driving your car today?"

"No one drives my car but me."

"Was there anyone else driving your car today?"

"Do you know what?" I snapped. And before he could utter another word, I exploded. "You are a goddamn racist." I paused, my fury rising up from deep in my belly. Fear of getting arrested had turned to fury at his presumption. "I wonder how many other black men you've harassed today. You're the enemy of all black people!"

Forced to consider his own undoing, something in him went numb, and he took a couple of steps back. He gestured toward me. "Calm down! I'm just doing my job here. This is an investigation. Your race has nothing to do with it."

"You are a racist!" I snarled. I had had enough putting up with his incredible stupidity. "The woman in the bank told you I'm not the guy. Why are you still following me around, asking about my brother driving this car?"

He froze, staring.

"If you intend to arrest me for something I had nothing to do with, go ahead. Take me in!" I extended my hands out the window in his direction. I was not sure what I was saying; my dignity was violated. I was incensed. "There's a reason why so many black men are in jail."

He knew he was wrong. No one betrays their own conscience and escapes unscathed. An unjust attack takes down the assailant with the victim.

"No," he said, his voice clipped. "You're all set."

"Wait a minute," I said, my anger inciting me to act more boldly. "I need your badge number." I reached over and opened the glove compartment and grabbed a pen and paper. I wrote down his name too.

Unfazed, he simply returned to his patrol car and got in behind the wheel.

Like some wounded bird, I looked over at the old man.

"So what was that all about?" the old man said. "What did he want?"

"He wanted to arrest me for some crime at the bank."

"May God protect you from him," he said, pulling out his thick black prayer beads and beginning to move his lips in silent prayer.

The house of God is where black bodies have gathered for four hundred years to curse the crimes of the white man, and yet still the Almighty has not sent down his retribution for these assaults against weak and tired black bodies.

"Prayers won't do anything against white savagery," I murmured to myself in my anger. "But bullets and bloodshed might do some good."

Yet I knew even in that moment that violence was not a solution. My life had been a chronicle of war. My father slept with a gun, as his father and his father's father had done. I did not want that for myself. Guns were meant for death. Guns create nothing and destroy everything.

No poet can carry a gun and keep his talent.

I never reported the incident. I never talked about it with anyone else. You see, if you remain silent, white people will never know your pain and thus be able to label you a trouble-maker.

You are safe, but in accepting an inferior status, your self-regard suffers.

On the other hand, if you speak up and fight back, you uncover your restlessness and discontent, and white people will then persecute you for your resistance and ultimately destroy you as an example for other blacks to take note of.

Either way, you're condemned.

Found guilty.

23

IN THE AMERICAN SUBURBS, LIFE WAS CALM.

All I saw were suburban Americans who thought of themselves as white.

Black Americans walking, jogging, or biking were a rarity, but there were a few working at McDonald's and Papa Gino's and in other food stores in town.

The only time I saw black people was in the morning as they got off the bus to go to work and in the evening, as they got back on the bus to go home. Even today, black people are kept in low-paying jobs as cheap labor. Just as it did in the days of slavery, America profits from this cheap labor.

The leaves turned yellow and then fell from the trees, ushering in the fall season. I woke up early, brushed my teeth, took a shower, went to the kitchen, and made a peanut butter sandwich. Then, before I realized it, it was time to grab my backpack, jump in my car, and ride to the library.

Oh, how I enjoyed my morning ride through those clean, quiet streets with hardly anyone out walking. Arriving at the library, I parked the car and jumped out.

I walked into the library and sought out the perfect spot to spend the day reading, a place to hide and work on mastering the language.

Pulling out *The Autobiography of Malcolm X*, I tucked myself into a corner and began to read. It was Mrs. Parker, a black high-school counselor, who had suggested I read it. I had already been reading about the black man in America, so I was open to her suggestion.

Mrs. Parker was not my high-school teacher, nor was she assigned to me as a counselor. Rather, she was in charge of busing black students from Boston to this white suburban town. She loved black people.

On her own, she took it upon herself to teach me, to give me Malcolm's autobiography as a gift, to help me learn to understand my new reality in white America. The America of cops chasing black men in the streets of Boston and Chicago, New York and Minneapolis.

"Have you heard of Brother Malcolm?" she asked, excited to share new knowledge.

"No," I confessed, clueless about the history of black struggle in America.

"I'm sure you haven't seen this book before," she continued. "It's one of the most remarkable books to come out of the movement here in America."

"Mm-hmm." I nodded. I had no inkling of what she was talking about.

"In Africa, you are African. But in America, you are African American."

"I understand," I said, more out of respect than agreement.

"No, my brother," she said. "I can tell you don't understand what I'm talking about."

"Mm-hmm," I murmured again.

I could see she was clever and could read my face.

"The way white people portray us in the media is all you have access to in Africa. I understand. It's not your fault, because we don't control the media. That's just the way it is. Whenever you see people like us in the movies, they are all thugs and drug dealers."

It was true that I had thought I knew something about the life of black people in America from watching movies. When I was young in Mogadishu, my friends and I used to sit next to each other on a bamboo mat and watch our neighbor's nineteen-inch Magnavox tabletop television as black bodies appeared on the screen, portrayed as thugs and lazy people wearing hoodies, bandannas, and do-rags over their cornrows, sporting silver grills on their teeth and sweatbands on their wrists.

There they stood, lurking in dark alleyways. As some random vehicle drove by, they emerged with pistols and robbed people. Or again, we watched black women holding drinks and dancing in the clubs, wearing sexy denim shorts. Some were visibly drunk, and others were grinding up against strange men.

Growing up in Mogadishu, we were fed these images, the portrait of a people with no community, no faith, not an atom of family values.

By the time I met Mrs. Parker, my knowledge of blacks in America was distorted, and I had no idea how to decipher the truth. Mrs. Parker was pointing out that the Hollywood image I brought with me from Africa originated in an unprecedented conquest of black bodies, in a massive seizure of African culture and religion, in a flagrant expropriation of African knowledge.

The European conquest of Africa had conceived those distorted images in my mind. Now, living in white America, I was unwittingly about to inherit that stolen legacy.

"I'm still struggling with the language," I said. "But I promise to read any and all of the books you give me."

"Reading will give you access to the reality of this country. If I had another country to go to, like you, I wouldn't make any claim that this country is ours."

"Yes." I nodded. The home I knew in Africa was no more.

I felt that destiny had carried me on its back and dropped me here in this suburban town with perfectly trimmed green grass, with paved roads where dogs jogged with their owners, and with birds flying low and high without any fear of the humans below.

A town where men pushing green and red lawn mowers cut the grass and trimmed the trees as if they were giving haircuts. A town where cold and hot water was democratic.

A town where boys played American football and girls played tennis and volleyball.

A town where old people wore their Sunday best to the church next to the fire station, the high school, and the library. America, I had come to think, was where I belonged, the home I was searching for. And I did not want Mrs. Parker's vision of America to spoil it for me. But still I thought I understood her words somewhat, because I had already glimpsed bigotry in America, but my heart refused the portrait she was painting.

I had lost the country of my childhood. And now, because of what Mrs. Parker was trying to teach me, I was losing my adopted country.

My mind was clouded.

But as I write this today, everything Mrs. Parker said to me lingers, inescapable, as honest and clear as a cloudless sky. I see her sitting on a chair in her office. Her smooth dark skin. Her hair is short. She is wearing glasses. Her voice is scratchy, as if worn out from overuse in the struggle.

The more I read the *Autobiography*, the more I thought about my father, fighting the colonial powers in Somalia. On the morning my father took his last breath and died in front of me—that very morning—he spoke about how he had witnessed the loss of his family in those wars. His father and mother and five brothers were all dead.

He himself became a fighter at the tender age of fourteen.

My mother thought that my father died of cancer, but he came back sick from fighting in Africa's perpetual colonial wars. He lost his life struggling for freedom, and so did Malcolm—Brother Malcolm, as Mrs. Parker used to call him. With uncompromising honesty, they risked everything they held dear so that others might live in dignity and with the respect they deserved.

My father and Malcolm were the first to teach me that you need to understand your own humanity, the struggle within, before you can take your rightful place in the world. If you can survive war and exile, slavery and Jim Crow, you can shape your destiny. But you cannot alter it.

Hardship creates character possibilities and spiritual aptitude, but destiny determines the course of your life. Destiny led me to Mrs. Parker. Destiny made me a black man living in America. When destiny winks, claps, and moves its wings, I sense something of its direction.

If I did not believe in destiny, I would end up in the madhouse.

24

I AM AT WORK, SITTING AT MY DESK, WHEN THE PHONE RINGS.
Years have gone by, and now another one is passing. I am thinking of this job as a career. Not looking at the phone ID, I pick it up.

"Hello," I say.

"Hello," Deric replies. "Is this Boyah?"

"Yes," I reply. "Speaking. Don't you recognize my voice?"

"Not really," he says. "Your files are here. You can come and get them."

"Thank you. I'm coming."

I leave my cubicle and head for Deric's office. Just outside in the hallway, I see him holding the files and standing with some other black coworkers, and I join them. As we stand there, greeting one another, Williams, a black colleague of ours, strolls by.

He glances slyly at us and then whispers conspiratorially under his breath, "You know what they say about black folks standing around together in the hallway?" Then he dashes off, smiling.

Sasha, a colleague, nods to me. "Did you get that?"

She is a black woman with a deep Caribbean accent, strong

as steel, and has worked with me in the company over many years. Her reputation for efficiency, diligence, and ethical standards follows her. She has always been good to me.

"Not really," I say. "What's he talking about?"

"If you don't get it, I guess you haven't really lived long enough in America." She grins. "The white people haven't gotten to you yet and made you black like us."

"What are you talking about?"

"You probably don't know much about what we have to go through here. You're African, but you're not black. Not yet."

Now I smile. "After living and working here since I was a teenager, experiencing the deep river of American racism, don't you think white America has taught me what it is to be black?"

"You're so full of shit," she says, smiling. "But I like that river metaphor of yours. Your language is always so beautiful."

Whenever anyone compliments me on how I use words, they think they're just saying something nice—and they are—but they don't know how deeply satisfying it is to me. It feels like confirmation of my status, coming from the nation of poets. Her words seem to carry the weight of an oracle.

"Your point is well taken," says another black man with broad shoulders, standing with the group. "White folks are always watching you." Clearly, he knows something that I have yet to learn.

"If you ask me, nothing changes," a petite black woman with long hair says. "If you want to keep your job, then stay focused on what they tell you. Shut your mouth and simply pretend you are a fly on the wall."

"That's true," says a black man with dreadlocks. "But we need to be like Harriet Tubman and Susan B. Anthony, so we can resist, struggle, and change this." Listening to the group, I understand them, but it is beyond anything I can imagine to allow another man to control me. As they speak, I am still thinking about what Sasha said.

"Thanks for the compliment, Sasha, but I'm serious. What exactly is he saying about black folk?"

"Well, in the old days, if a white person saw three or four black people standing around talking together, they were suspected of plotting against the whites."

"But that all happened back during slavery. This is the twenty-first century."

"Your eyes don't see clearly yet. You're an unlearned African brother. America teaches us all in due time. You will learn about America, Boyah."

I chuckle. "America may be trying to put me in my place, but I don't accept where America wants me to go. I will never accept mental slavery."

"We'll see. It might take longer with you, but you will eventually."

As I take the files from Deric, he looks at me with a grin on his lips. "That's the same thing I've been telling you all along."

"Yeah, I know," I say. "I remember you telling me the same thing Sasha just said."

"Boy," he whispers. "Eventually, you'll learn." As he walks away, the group disperses, and I amble back to my office, lost in thought.

I always had the feeling that I belonged in America, but now I am feeling alone. When I arrived here, the English language didn't belong to me. My taste buds didn't yet belong to America. Burgers, fried chicken, hot dogs, and pancakes were still foreign to me, but I was eager to assimilate my tastes and my words to America. My mother wore African dresses and cooked rice or spaghetti with goat meat, while America expected me to behave like one of her own black men, steeped in her history. My gaze was busy recording into my memory everything new and foreign. When I was forced to survive in this complicated new culture, it came naturally to me to behave as a fearless African warrior. Once at home in America, I sat with my family and watched stacks of videos about Africa—that place in my spirit that was left behind, but still lingered.

Sitting in my cubicle, I consider the snow falling outside the window, but inside the lights are bright. I lose myself in looking at the snowflakes, drifting and floating and melting in midair, or piling up over the green grass. All is calm and silent; snow covers everything below. Then my boss, Blake, a white man with protruding ears, walks into my cubicle, interrupting my thoughts.

"Did you get your coffee?" Blake says, standing over me.

"Yes, I did. I can't live without coffee in the morning."

"I completely understand."

"I confess, I'm really addicted to coffee."

"Look, I see your friend Deric is in here all the time."

"Don't you think 'all the time' is just a bit of an exaggeration? He only comes to me when he has a question."

"He can't keep coming into the back office, Boyah. If he needs your help, let him stand at the window like everyone else, and the clerks can help him out."

"Okay, but he's an employee too. What did Deric do that was wrong?"

"I never said he did anything wrong. What I'm telling you to do is to stop him from coming in the back behind the clerk's window and sitting in your cubicle."

"Is this a new policy? Does this apply to everyone? What's the reasoning here?"

"You don't need any reasoning. Just don't let him come back in your cubicle, okay? It's totally up to you to do what I ask. You're okay. You're different because you're smart. Right now, everyone likes you. You're good."

"Thanks," I say, uneasy.

"I'm sure you know what I'm talking about. If he has a question for you, let him ask you at the window."

"Okay, Blake. But let me ask you something."

"Of course." He folds his hands patiently.

"Is this new—a new policy? Does this apply to all employees?"

"It's totally up to you. You're free to do or not to do what I'm asking."

"I'm not going to stop him from coming to my cubicle with questions. I couldn't do it, even if I wanted to! He hasn't done anything to me!"

Blake turns and steps away. My refusal has upset him. My stomach begins to gurgle. My armpits itch. I stand up and step out into the hallway so I can process Blake's demand and the reprimand I know is coming because of my refusal. Deric's and Sasha's warnings are beginning to weigh on me, beginning to hit home. And yet I am still a bit confused. America has been good to me, and I cannot betray her. But she has betrayed generations of black people for centuries before my arrival, and she seems destined to betray me as well. Shall I pretend and follow Blake's instructions, or shall I maintain my integrity without compromise? People throughout the world use family, wealth, and religion to separate and deny one another. But I thought America would be different.

When I was little, I once sat with my father outside our home. The sun was falling. The pigeons were pecking in the brown sand, looking for invisible grains. The neighborhood monkey was sitting in the branches of a large tree inside the courtyard of the house next door. An old lady was standing on a mat as she prayed. Visible in the distance, boys were playing soccer in the field, dust rising under their running feet. My father was wearing his army uniform, with a gun on his shoulder and a water bottle and pistol in his large army belt. My mother was at work selling goods in the market. As he sat, my father placed his gun between his legs. Pulling out a cigarette, he lit and puffed once, twice. My tiny eyes followed the smoke leaving his lips and nose and then rising and falling over his face and melting in the air. I was younger then; and as I watched the smoke from his cigarette, I imagined to myself that I would, one day, place a cigarette between my lips and puff and release smoke into the air like him. My father was a revolutionary man, and I wanted to be just like him.

"Look, my son," he said to me. "You are nothing without your words."

"I understand you," I replied. I didn't really understand him, but I was afraid. His words and his actions and his voice soared as I sat next to him. I feared him and then I adored him, for he was an African man who had endured despite so much trauma in his life.

"Never break your word for anyone," he said. "Never betray your soul. Stay honest. Wear your conviction until your last breath." What he told me, I try to practice, and I never break my word to anyone. I remember who I am and what I shall always remain: an African nomad with dark-shaded skin who never compromises and who never allows a white American to reduce me to the man of their imagination. I refuse to be used. I am a free man. My imagination is free. My spirit is free. My soul is free. My finances may rest in the hands of white people at work, but my dignity remains with me forever, while the long-term value of money is passing.

I must work, not only to afford basic living expenses but to maintain my manhood, my self-respect. If my job is taken away, what human worth will I have? Freedom does not mean just walking around and smiling and dancing—no, freedom means working to protect your family from being thrown out in the street. You can sing about America all you want, but if you cannot provide for a roof over your body or buy food for your family, you are not free.

There is nothing I can do to alter this situation for myself, but I still have legs to walk. I step into the bathroom and stand in front of the mirror and begin to splash my face with cold water, over and over again, trying to dissipate my frustration. As I feel more composed, I walk outside. Standing there, alone and peering into the falling snow, part of me wishes that I could be as free as that snow gently falling from the sky. My body may be intact, but my spirit and the thoughts inside me are hurting. I feel trapped.

Blake wants to control who comes into my cubicle, and it is clear that it is the black people he wants to keep from me. He is watching me. He is testing me. But I feel distant from him. I am outside, thinking and feeling as if I were standing—head bowed, hair wild, shirt ripped—in front of a judge reading a guilty verdict, guilty for the shade of my skin, no longer free.

I am losing control of my spinning mind. My thoughts are running wild.

Within the deepest chamber of my heart festers a profound

spiritual dislocation. Having struggled with disease and hunger and death, I owe my life to America. But as much as I hate to admit it, I am physically free, but threatened with enslavement. Can my love for America justify letting her take ownership of my life? Am I really only an alien outsider—no longer African, but in America not yet black?

Suddenly I feel a bit dizzy, lightheaded. My knees feel weak.

Deric and I are not brothers. We do not share the same cultural experience or outlook. But as we walk down this road together and exchange greetings as we pass, America is making us brothers, closer than blood.

Wondering what it would take to release my strangled mind and looking for something to take my mind away from the moment, I begin mindlessly to count the cars parked in the lot.

At my age, I am certainly old enough to know myself and my situation.

I slip my hand into my back pants pocket and pull out a pen. I look around and spot a piece of paper drifting in the wind. I run after it, grab it, and write down some words.

Dad. Father. Abo,
When your body
Decays
And decomposes
And drifts
I am
Your son,
First one.
Your living words are in me.
I can stand
Or run

Or swim
Or walk
And fight
And defend,
Or speak up
For the weak,
For the family,
For the valley,
Anywhere,
Everywhere,
In God's land.
I am equal
To all
Humanity,
No words for my America.
I am an unlearned black man.
America is showing me its ways,
For I am a student in its belly.

25

ONE YEAR ON THE JOB REPLACES ANOTHER.

Trump replaces Obama. Hope is replaced by headaches and despair.

More and more, I don't feel well. My head hurts. I can't control my thoughts. My stomach is upset. Sleepless nights are becoming routine. I am not sure what is wrong with me. I have a recurring headache.

I decide to email Blake and tell him that I will be taking a sick day.

That morning starts with despairing tears in my eyes and ends with a long night of battle, my mind looping endlessly, as if it were a car stuck in the snow, wheels spinning. The feeling eats up my insides. I hope that sleep might provide temporary relief. Tossing, turning, cussing all night in bed, I get up, rub my eyes, grab my iPhone, jump on YouTube, turn on some relaxing music, and lay my head back down on the pillow with my headphones. But the engine inside my head refuses to slow down.

It accelerates and produces nothing but burnout.

Waking up, I sit down in the living room and turn on the television.

After twenty-five minutes, I go to the kitchen, open the

drawer, find a bottle of melatonin, and toss two tablets in my mouth. I take three steps over to the fridge, grab its door, pull out a gallon of milk, and pour some into a cup. I gulp down the tablets, meditating on distant Africa. In Somalia, when families from the same neighborhood started killing each other, I was twelve years old.

Back then, I saw dead people in the street, but I did not cry.

When the girl who was my childhood crush was shot dead, execution-style, right in front of my eyes, even then I did not cry. A bitter taste of saliva gathers in my mouth. I spit it out until I throw up.

"Oh, good grief," I shout out loud, swallowing hard the bad-tasting milk.

What keeps me from closing my eyes is bigger than anything else I have ever faced in my life. My father was a fighter, a combatant in the Somali national army, and he battled bravely for his freedom. He impressed upon me that my real enemy was the enemy within the soul.

I can never forget that woman with her very thin waist, her chiseled face and big eyes, her bright red dress and matching scarf. She was shot and killed. Nor can I forgive myself for the young man in his twenties who was stoned to death before my very eyes on the beach in the coastal city of Kismayo. When white particles oozed out of his skull, I felt a lump in my stomach. I crouched down, dropped to my knees in the sand, faced the vast Indian Ocean, and threw up.

I even saw a man with one leg sitting near a hospital, shouting as if he had lost his mind. A lone militiaman ordered him to shut up.

The crippled man refused, crying out, "Get it over with and shoot me!"

The militiaman drew his gun, placed it on the crippled man's forehead, and fired two bullets. The cripple fell onto the sand like a piece of cement. I flinched and ducked.

I felt bad for the man, but again I did not cry. Once his soul left him and his body ceased shivering, his pain was over. I knew that, and I was happy for him.

One early morning I stepped out and saw a dead body lying in the street. There was gunfire in the air, and gray clouds were covering the sun. Two men were digging a hole in the ground for the corpse lying nearby, and out of fear for my own demise, I thought to join them. I started digging along with them.

We dug a shallow hole, dropping in the lifeless body and burying it.

The air smelled of fresh blood.

When I heard a wail, I craned my neck and saw blood oozing out of another man's torso. He wailed, and his body moved, but I pretended not to see. When he wailed again, I saw that his eyes remained steadily open, and I imagined that his soul was drifting upward.

All that was many years ago.

American color prejudice, unseen and unexamined, I find much more painful. Intangible and disembodied, it begins as if it were a nothing, a silent killer, but slowly it seeps into my bloodstream, breathes into my lungs, stabs at my heart, and morphs into this endless nightmare.

It makes me upset at the whole world. It even plays with my taste buds so that I eat less.

It decays in my mind, gives me a vicious headache, and upsets my stomach—like love.

Only this time it isn't love. The contaminating rot of malice occupies my body.

The next morning, it is freezing outside. Getting ready to go to work, I put on a T-shirt, jeans, and shoes. The office dress code is casual, but dressing in clothes I like doesn't make me feel anywhere near relaxed. An unknown danger is moving and eating parts of my belly.

I grab my car keys. I like cars and enjoy driving the freeways. Driving gives me freedom.

I climb in my car and rev the engine.

And then I spin out of the parking lot, careening along the city's main road. Instead of heading toward the office, however, I find myself driving down the highway, heading somewhere I don't recognize and belting out Tupac's "Only God Can Judge Me," a song that continues to be a favorite of mine, no matter how far beyond rap my musical interests have traveled. I keep my love for music hidden from my mother and brothers because music is my access to America. Soul stirring, but contradictory. Healing, but destructive.

I cut in between two cars and move along at a high speed.

In my rearview mirror, I watch them almost collide.

Something unknown is eating parts of me. I think I know what it is, but I just can't put my finger on it. It is something much greater than me, greater than my family, greater than my culture. It is something as American, so to speak, as apple pie.

Despite my ten years in the workforce, I am new to this feeling, and my entire being is driven to resist. As I accelerate, the pain eases, and I am free, temporarily better.

By the time I glance down at the speedometer, I am doing well over a hundred miles per hour, fast approaching nowhere and everywhere.

I see nothing but cars, hills, trees, snow, random houses, and endless pavement stretching ahead. Freedom for my soul.

I begin to reflect. Speeding to escape my hurt, I am lost now out on the highway.

"Damn," I mutter to myself. "I must be losing my mind."

I pull over near some woods. Rolling down the window, I let myself feel the cool breeze rushing onto my face as I tilt my head up, staring at the gray sky.

"It's nothing," I remind myself. "If I survived that bloody war, I can survive anything."

I chant that aloud again, like a Tupac rap. I sense a hint of the lie in my words.

But the truth is, right then I really need to lie to myself, to ease my pain.

"Hell, I'm the only black man here, for God's sake," I tell myself.

Turning back onto the highway and speeding off to work, I keep talking to myself. "My black tribe isn't around. Aren't Blake and his ilk all part of that other tribe, that white tribe?"

At last, I park in the company lot, but I linger inside my car.

"My boss is white. His boss is white. Everyone's boss is white. Isn't that the same tribe?"

Stepping out of the car, I climb the hill, passing through the revolving front door, and enter the large main office, finding my cubicle. When my stomach rumbles and shifts, I drag myself to the bathroom.

In front of the mirror, I see an image of myself looking back at me. I am a survivor.

My face, widening. My night sleep, vanishing. My eyes, red. My hair, thinning.

As a member of the human family, I know that part of me belongs to Blake and his white tribe, but I see myself as another black body, harassed and belittled. The part of me that belongs to them is condemned to cry and sweat in protest against their crimes. My body is weak. My thoughts are blurred.

I'm trapped in America like a caged bird.

I am prediabetic. Deric tells me that he too is prediabetic. The stress from being a black man in America is to blame for our declining health. I am emotionally suffocating, like an old man struggling for air, as my life collapses around me.

Despite the emotional turmoil residing in me, I always appreciate the small and almost meaningless things in life—my breathing, taking a dump in the toilet without hardship, chewing a piece of meat and then swallowing and feeling chunks of food rolling down and passing through my throat before resting somewhere in my belly. I always smile humbly when seeing the sky or feeling the falling rain, because I know that I can lose them all at once.

"That's nice," I murmur to myself, looking in the mirror, recalling how nice and easy it is for me to use the bathroom. "I like that."

"Is that you, Boyah?" Deric's voice echoes from one of the toilet stalls. "Why are you standing there talking to yourself like some weirdo?"

"Yeah, Deric," I respond. "It's me. Stop talking and finish your business. I'll wait for you."

Deric comes out of the toilet next to me. Both of us face the mirror, examining ourselves. Deric is a large man, taller than I. Our skin tones shade into the same black.

As Deric washes up, I stand next to him, drying my face with paper towels.

"So, Boyah," he says. "What's up?"

"Nothing," I lie. "You know what?"

"What?" He takes two steps toward me. "What's wrong with you?"

"I just looked at myself in the mirror. I'm aging."

"Really!" he says sarcastically. "Aging is the last thing you need to worry about. You're becoming a black man in America now."

"What are you saying?"

"You know the stress from this job can kill you," he says. "I know it sure is killing me."

"I'm not so sure about that," I reply. "I am indestructible. Remember, I survived war."

"Maybe so, but that was back in Africa," he says. "You're in America now."

"Huh." I smile. "Your America is teaching me something."

"My America." He smiles too. "America is our nightmare, and we are now in this together." As he and I smile, cheering ourselves, he walks out of the bathroom and I follow him. We end up sitting in his office, still chatting about America and our plight on the job.

Megan pops into his office.

"Where have you been this morning?" she barks, annoyed, pulling her wild blond hair back into a low ponytail, frowning.

"I've been right here all morning," Deric replies evenly.

"No, you haven't," Megan challenges him. "I came to your office just a moment ago and couldn't find you. You were no-where around."

"Just now, I was in the restroom, but I've been here all morning. You probably came by when I took a break."

As they face off, I am fascinated by how genuinely vexed her expression appears. As she chastises him like a little boy, she ignores me, sitting there listening. Perhaps she wants me to take note, so I can understand this America of hers where white people dominate.

"Someone was just looking for you," she says in a snotty, bossy tone. "Stop taking these long breaks all the time. Remember, you took a sick day off yesterday, and now you really have a lot of work to make up. No one around here is going to do your job."

"I was sick yesterday, but I've been catching up this morning," Deric contends.

"Yeah, but I really need you to do your job and get this work done," she says. "You understand, don't you?"

"Yes," Deric murmurs.

The scene is brutal.

I have never seen Megan bother any of the white coworkers in the office. I have never seen her take them to task when they call out sick or waltz in and out of the office at their leisure. I have never heard her breathe a single word about their outrageous and unprofessional behavior. The white coworkers indulge themselves freely. Megan reminds me of Blake, who practices similar behavior. It's as if they took a chapter from the same book on America's subjection of the black people.

It is unbearable.

Megan is indifferent to my presence. Her stare is cold, bitter, contemptuous, blank, and silent. As Deric's world is falling apart in front of me, mine is heading in the same direction. Oh, boy, isn't life a painful ordeal?

I soon regret staying behind to witness Megan's humiliation of Deric.

"I was really disappointed with your last presentation," she says. "You didn't do what I asked you to do. I'm disappointed."

He is bewildered. "I'm sorry. What didn't I do?"

"You didn't do a competent job on your last presentation."

"But I showed you my notes. What did I do wrong?"

Megan lectures him: he was late; he wasn't professional; he was not representing the office very well.

Deric tries to object, but Megan brooks no discussion. "More and more, I'm finding that you aren't getting your work done," she says, finishing him off. Then she strides away in a huff while Deric and I sit blinking at each other.

"Welcome to the Negro's life at work," Deric says gravely, shaking his head.

"Yeah," I whisper, nodding. "I'm in the same boat."

Justifying her behavior to himself, Deric dismisses the incident as Megan attempting to produce a "teachable moment." He is lying to himself and contradicting his own experience by thinking that she wants to help him improve with her criticism. The complexity of what we are facing is beyond us.

"So," I say, "what are you going to do?"

"What can I do?" Deric says, desperately sad.

"You should have defended yourself and questioned her right there on the spot about her own pathetic conduct."

"I try." He sighs. "But, you know, when these white people are wrong, they don't apologize or change."

"But she's wrong," I say, raising my voice. "I know they're not going to do anything about it, but you still need to let the world hear your voice."

"Uh, well," Deric says, shaking his head. "Maybe I will make a complaint about her."

"That's great," I say brightly. I feel convoluted thoughts boiling up within me. "But we need to do more. Let the world know about this."

"Hey, look, you don't know how these white folks protect one another. Nothing's going to come from these complaints."

Oh, for sure, I'm well versed in their tribal ways, but I am African. I am resolved to remain exactly who and what I am: a warrior.

But I see my future in Deric's present.

26

SOMETIME AFTER OUR CONFRONTATION, BLAKE HIRES A WHITE woman. Although the position requires a bachelor's degree, Heather has only a high-school diploma. Yet Blake somehow has managed to have the requirement waived for her.

One day, he brings her around the office to introduce her to everyone and show her to her cubicle near mine. She is a young brunette, a white woman in her early thirties, with highlights in her long hair. Under her right arm is a spiral notebook. She pauses in front of me and looks directly into my eyes.

"So, how long have you been on the job here?"

"Ten years or so," I reply. "Maybe eleven years, I suppose."

Her eyes remain locked on mine, and I find this very strange, curious.

Blake gestures to Heather to move on and begins to step over to her cubicle. I follow them with my eyes and listen as Blake shows her to her new office space.

He points to the empty wall space and remarks, "Hang up whatever you want here, pictures of the family, anything."

"Great," she says.

"I guess you noticed that Boyah's got nothing to hang on his office wall," he jokes. "Right, Boyah?" he says in a staged voice, loud enough for me to hear him.

I blink. "I don't like hanging things up on the wall."

Blake and Heather laugh together. I don't feel at home here, so why should I personalize my office space?

Later that week, Heather pins up a photo of her mother and father holding hands as the Eiffel Tower looms behind them. In another picture, the same couple is in front of Saint Peter's Basilica at the Vatican.

Sitting in my cubicle next to hers, I can see Heather personalizing her cubicle. I nod to her, although I feel no emotion. I just want to get away. She puts up a picture of her cat and wants to show it to me. So I smile and take a quick look. The other object on her wall is an American flag.

"I hate it when people disrespect our flag," she announces proudly, pointing to the red, white, and blue. "The greatest flag of the greatest country on earth. Isn't that so, Boyah?"

I just smile. She is echoing Donald Trump's denunciation of Colin Kaepernick taking a knee during the national anthem in 2016 to protest police brutality and racial inequality. We are much too busy around the office to think about flags or the toxic bombast of Trump-era politics.

I also ignore her bragging, "I don't have an associate's degree, and I still got the job." To hear her tell it, she is overqualified, even without the prerequisite college credential. She used to sell clothes in a mall department store, and now, thanks to Blake's intervention, she enjoys a big, clean cubicle of her own, with a good salary, benefits, and job security.

White people under Blake do exceptionally well. He gives

them salary increases and promotions to better positions. Non-whites he treats as aliens, constantly searching for a quick way to remove them. In fact, during all my years here, I have never seen a single white employee let go.

Strangely, though, despite Blake playing favorites, Heather doesn't really like the job. One day, in fact, she goes AWOL, doesn't show up, just vanishes.

For a week, no one hears from her.

After the first day or two of Heather's no-shows, Blake ambles over to my cubicle. It is the morning of the organization's annual meeting. "Have you heard from Heather?" he asks.

In a state of bewilderment, I blink. "No. I don't know her like that." As a flag-hugger, she is as vain as Trump. I know not to mess with Heather.

He glowers icily at me. "But aren't you friends with her on Facebook?"

Many filthy words dance in my mind, but I am not going to let those words shoot off my lips. I just give him a blank stare. "Sorry," I say. "Barely know her."

Moving away, he goes from cubicle to cubicle, asking all ten employees if they have any information regarding Heather's whereabouts.

About a week later, wearing a long-sleeved white top with a black skirt, Heather pops back in to work. And not only that, but after just ten months on the job, she is promoted to a position that earns her more money than many of us with longer tenure.

One morning, as I push through the revolving front door, I hear Blake call out behind me. I wait, and we walk down the hall and into the office together. Someone in another department has brought over leftover birthday pizza, so I smile and open up my mouth.

As we eat, Blake looks at me as if he is about to say something important. "I have good news for you," Blake says, hovering over the boxes of pizza.

Looking up to hear the good news, I chew and listen.

"There's a new job opening up that I think you should apply for."

"Oh?" Interested, I put down the pizza, feeling like I am drowning in my own saliva. But the position he is suggesting I apply for pays worse than mine. If I were to get the job, I would no longer be working under him. "Really? I'm not looking for a demotion."

"It's just a suggestion," Blake says. "Think about it."

I'm sure he senses a crackle of annoyance in the tone of my words, so he just walks away. My thoughts spin and swirl. I can't eat anymore.

Despite working here for over ten years and helping hundreds of clients, I am unwanted.

After everyone leaves for the day, I stay behind in my cubicle.

Something has sparked in my mind, and the need to write wells up in me.

Dear Blake,

I worked hard today, but you ruined it for me. Just for a moment I would like you to imagine our roles reversed. Imagine if I were your boss, and one day after you worked really hard, rather than show gratitude, I told you to find another job. How would you feel? Wouldn't it damage your dignity? But if you intended to fracture my sense of self-worth, you failed. My dignity remains intact. Please respect my work and my worth as a fellow human being.

Thank you.
Boyah

The following Monday, I walk into my cubicle and see Blake sitting there, waiting. Never before has he ever bothered to come talk to me in my cubicle space. I always have to go to him, so I wonder what the significance of this is.

"Good morning," I say.

"I just wanted to tell you I am sorry," he begins.

"About what?" I ask.

"Last Friday. You misunderstood my suggestion. I really thought you might be a good fit for the position I suggested to you."

Trying to understand the truth behind his apology, I scrutinize his face.

"Blake." I sigh. "You really make life difficult for me around here."

"What do you mean? I'm not trying to get rid of you. I'm just trying to suggest a better position for you."

"I was called into your boss's office last week, and she showed me that you have been writing me up for silly complaints that have nothing to do with my job performance. On top of that, you never take any time to train me or explain why you think I'm not doing a good job. So I know that you don't want me here. You know it, and I know it, Blake. You're part of a much larger problem here. It's only black people you fire for incompetence."

"That's not true," he responds defensively, drawing his legs closer together. His cheeks turn red, and sweat glistens on his forehead. "I have no clue what you're trying to say, Boyah. I merely came in here to apologize. I was only suggesting you apply for a position that I thought you might enjoy more."

"The issue at hand is not your suggestion. It's how you treat black employees. I know that eventually you will succeed in getting me out of here, but I'm not afraid of you, and my destiny is secure. But in the meantime, what I need from you is respect, because the one thing I do not compromise is my dignity. If it is meant for me to be fired, so be it."

At that, Blake gets up and storms out. At that moment, one thing is clear: he is pathetic. His smiles are not genuine, only deception in disguise. Judging from his actions toward me, I know he considers blacks in the company incompetent, whatever their position. I am the enemy he has to neutralize by sidling up to and trying to get closer to. It's a game I refuse to play. That's not what I want for my life. My father was right when he told me that there was wisdom in the progression of time. Time is teaching me.

I am a changed man now. When I first got this job, I was a free human being. But the terror I taste every day when I walk through those doors and come into that office does not belong to me. It was designed four hundred years earlier, and it is inherited and maintained by people who smile each time they see you in the corridor. But after they smile at you, they go back to their office and try to figure out how to remove you.

I'm thinking of quitting, but I don't know how. I have been at this job for over ten years. The job is like a marriage you know is finished but still can't walk away from because you have invested so many years into the relationship. I wonder if the job is worth the battle.

From that day, Blake and I never speak again meaningfully, other than to nod a greeting or mutter a word about the weather.

I am heading toward clinical depression.

When Blake leaves my cubicle, I walk over to the records office to search for a file. The door is locked, so I knock. A white colleague in his forties opens the door and pokes his head out. Seeing me, he holds up his hand, blocking me from entering.

"Sorry, you can't come in here," he says forcefully.

"What do you mean?"

"I don't want you taking anything out of here."

"What are you trying to say?" I ask politely.

"I don't want you taking anything from here."

"Are you accusing me of trying to steal something?" I say flippantly, since I find what he is saying rather silly. "You think I'm a thief? What are you saying?"

"I don't have to be politically correct about what I'm trying to say," he says defiantly. "You're not getting in here. I don't want you taking even a pen from in here."

Maybe you shouldn't complain. This country adopted you and gave you an education, so of course you shouldn't complain. But how do you not complain when you're always fighting against everything—really, everything—because racism is so deeply ingrained in the social fabric of the country? Am I to think of myself as a little puppy or cat, some domesticated animal, and what would that mean, really? Is that what I have come to?

One day I see two men walk into Deric's office. They escort him out, carrying his belongings. I feel a pinch in my belly, and my mind kicks in. Deric has been fired. His gaze lowered from embarrassment, he glances up only for a moment and gives me a silent look, as if he were saying, *Look! They finally got me!* As he himself predicted, it is his destiny to lose this job at the hands of white people. My world is shrinking before me, but there is nothing I can do to alter the situation. This is Blake's world; Deric and I are nothing but scavenger scum. He is gone.

As the realization dawns on me, I rush to the bathroom and stand there. My stomach is moving, gurgling. My head is spinning. My eyes want to leak tears, but my nomad soul still will not let them flow freely. I am upset. I am hurt. I am watching my own fate in Deric's termination. Standing in the front of the mirror, I grab my phone and call him, but he refuses to pick up. Maybe it is shame. Or maybe it is America. Something inside him is telling him to shrink and disappear like others before him. Isn't our black skin a scarlet letter? For days, I call him and text him, but he never picks up or replies to any of my messages. I will never hear from him again. Later, I find out on Facebook that he has passed away from COVID-19.

America got Deric. I lost him to America. How many times do I have to lose something? First I lost my father and the dream of seeing him grow old and turn gray and pass on his wisdom to me. Then I lost the country of my birth, washed away in the blood of my childhood friends. And next I lost my very identity, my manhood, in the trimmed green grass of America. Deric is gone.

27

I WAKE UP WITH A LUMP IN MY THROAT.

I can't make out where it comes from. I call Dr. Sun, my doctor since high school, and go to see him in his office. I sit on the examination table.

He uncoils a gray stethoscope from his neck and places it on my chest. "So, tell me," he says. "You've been having a hard time sleeping?"

"I can't sleep. And there's some kind of lump in my throat."

"I don't see anything serious," he says as his cold hand touches my neck. He motions for me to turn my head. "Just to be sure, I'm going to refer you to a specialist."

"Thanks, Doctor. This not being able to sleep is just driving me crazy."

"Are you still working at the same job?"

"Yes."

I am fully aware of what is occupying my mind and body, but I can't tell him about that. I am too proud to complain about being reduced to an object for white people to harass.

This is their country. And although I've been here for many years, I still tell myself that one day I'll return to my homeland. Somalia has stabilized from the mayhem of tribal infighting, warlord domination, terrorism, and piracy. Northern Somalia is no longer a war zone. My family lives there. Hamud has recently returned to tell us all about his experiences with our *ayeyo*. He has learned to herd goats and milk them, drinking the unpasteurized milk. He has watched the slaughtering of sheep and goats, then eaten the cooked meat. No television or video games.

He has learned to meditate and look within himself, to grow as a person without the distractions he knew in America. His stories remind me of my childhood in the Nugaal Valley. I think to myself that I belong there.

Here, I am unable to find the source of my pain or smell it, but I hear its roar as it engulfs my mind, refuses me sleep, corners me in a tiny inhuman space where I crouch in front of the monotonous blue glare of the office computer, eight hours a day, five days a week.

"Any changes going on in your life, Boyah? Are you still writing?"

"Yes," I say.

"You're still writing about civil war in Africa?" I nod. "That must be painful."

"Yes." I don't have the stomach to complain about my white coworkers. "Maybe so."

"Maybe I can refer you to a good therapist."

"Thank you," I say. But my African upbringing kicks in. Something inside me refuses to see or talk to a therapist about not sleeping. Although I have been living in Boston for so many years, and even though I am now a naturalized American citizen, I still have buried inside me my father's African culture. "I'm not crazy."

Going to a therapist is beyond the pale, just not done.

"No, I didn't mean that," he says. "Seeing a good therapist would help you, so you can sleep better and even write better." He knows that I have been writing regularly for some years now.

"If a therapist can help me write better, then I guess I really should go."

"Yes, I think you really should."

"Sure," I say, succumbing out of respect.

I lose sleep that night, tossing and turning and cussing out Blake.

I swallow two goddamn tablets of sleeping pills with some bad milk. No dice. Nothing is working.

Impatient for the sunrise, wearing shorts and no shirt, I spend that night sitting in front of the television's flickering light, thinking of my life in ruins.

The next morning at Starbucks, it's my writing day. Thoughts of what I might write are exciting me as I sip my favorite dark roast coffee and stare for a while through the large glass window at all the vehicles moving through the snow outside. Then, as if automatically, the rhythm of writing visits me.

Unloading the pain onto the pages, I let those words talk back to me so I can learn something that eases my agitated soul.

I write like a child running and jumping and hopping through his favorite playground. I feel good about myself. In fact, every time I have a good writing day, I am happy, despite the painful beauty of living black in America. I want to write about America the way Karl Ove Knausgård writes about Norway. Like him, I would like to produce two thousand pages about my life.

By eleven o'clock, when I walk into the office at the start of my work shift, I am happy.

I pass the other employees and sit down at my desk. I adjust my chair and turn on the computer. As I sit looking at the monitor, I suddenly feel the shadow of Blake hovering over me. Before I can turn my head in his direction, I hear him speak.

"Boyah," he says, "Did you see that email from Human Resources?"

"No," I reply. "Not yet. I just got here—the computer is still loading up."

"You need to go to Human Resources right away."

As the words come out of his mouth, I tilt my head up to look into his eyes. But he quickly turns the other way to avoid my glance.

"Why?" I ask. "Am I in some kind of trouble?"

Inadvertently, I knock over the nearly empty Starbucks coffee cup sitting on my desk.

"Just go, you'll find out. And make sure you take your jacket and backpack with you."

The coffee cup is now upside down on the floor. A tiny cough escapes my mouth. I know where this is heading. However much I have been anticipating this moment, I find myself unprepared. "Am I getting fired?"

"Never mind. Just go upstairs. The HR director is waiting."

"Are you coming too?" I ask.

"Don't worry about me. Just make sure you go."

He knows he has the upper hand, and I have nothing but the glance of my pathetic eyes watching his demeanor. To his way of thinking, I am an insurrectionist or some kind of runaway slave. Grabbing my jacket and backpack, I walk out and turn to take the stairs up to the second-floor HR office, but my insides are sinking and pulling me down.

My head begins to hurt. My eyes blur. And as I lift my foot

onto the first step, my other foot refuses to follow. Then something pushes up in my throat, and my stomach turns. The air becomes thick as it coats my throat. My emotions are not so much agitated by the thought of losing the job. Rather, it's the feeling that I am being belittled and disparaged—as if I am nothing but a disposable black body. Turning away from the stairway, I enter the bathroom and stand in front of the mirror. I drop my backpack on the floor, turn the faucet on, and listen as the water runs. I then wash my hands and splash water on my face over and over again.

"So," I murmur to myself. "I guess I'm no different than Deric. But I know what I have to do. Whatever destiny has coming to me, I shall accept with grace and dignity."

But what kind of grace or dignity does a jobless man like me possess in capitalist America? I'm afraid and I'm naked and I'm not sure what to do with the fury rising and falling in me, the sharp sword cutting through my intestines.

My stomach. My eyes. My legs refuse to obey. My body is trembling. I feel like a prisoner. I may be physically free, but I can't move, and my mind belongs to Blake and his ilk. If God loves me, why must I endure this rejection and humiliation?

Since six o'clock this morning, I was sitting in my favorite spot at Starbucks, writing as if I were in love. I write to heal. I splash water on my face again, grab my backpack, and stretch. I step out of the bathroom bravely and say to myself out loud, "This is nothing."

I remember my mother's saying: "A man with a sense of humor is never at a loss for action."

I have survived war and bloodshed. I think of myself as unbreakable rock.

Then I remember one of my favorite Somali proverbs: "A

bridge is repaired only after someone falls in the water." I may be about to be fired, but I have the capacity to repair the bridge.

With that, I return to the stairwell, and this time my legs obey.

At the door of the HR office, I knock once softly.

"Come in," a woman says.

As I walk in, every one of the three white women sitting around the large conference table look up at me simultaneously. Blake is seated with them. He avoids my gaze.

My heart skips a beat.

"Have a seat, Boyah," the HR director says.

I sit down, but my mind is spinning with the thought that a coward dies before any of the courageous. I am getting fired, and I recognize it, but I am determined to remain true to myself.

"Do you know why you're here?"

Her eyes focus on me as if trained to cut through my body and intimidate my insides.

"No," I reply. My mind isn't mine anymore. My head is spinning. My stomach is churning.

"You are, in fact, on mandatory paid leave," she says. "And you will receive the results of our investigation by mail."

Poverty is slavery.

"You people have ruined many black lives," I say.

They look at one another with an air of disdain. Deep down in their hearts, I believe they know that what they are doing is wrong. Maybe on their deathbeds they will ask God for forgiveness.

"Am I free to leave now?" I ask.

"Yes, leave the building immediately."

With hunched shoulders and a feeling of defeat, I leave and return to the bathroom.

My kidneys ache as if they're full, but when I unzip my pants and attempt to urinate, nothing comes out. I return to the mirror but dare not look at my face, afraid to see my humiliation reflected back to me in the mirror. I step out and walk back to my cubicle.

Blake has returned to his office. I think I can glimpse a smirk on his face. I am upset, but my ego is happy that they have not called for security, like they did with Deric. I walk out of the office, turn down the stairs, and try to sneak out of the building.

At the building entrance, a black security guard sits observing me as if she expects my usual greeting. Feeling persecuted and vilified, I really don't want anyone to see me, and I slip by hoping to pass unnoticed. But she gets up from her seat, pokes her head out the door behind me, and waves. "So, you don't know how to say hi anymore? You're just going to pass by like that?"

"No," I say, unlocking the car door and starting to get in. "I just didn't see you." I turn on the car and take off. The turmoil roiling inside me is birthing a new reality that I need to process so that I can accept the shame and rejection and humiliation.

I feel numb. I need to work to pay for basic expenses like food, rent, heat, car, and insurance. To keep my self-respect. To preserve my dignity. But then I can't forgive myself for how I feel about losing my job. Allowing this job to occupy my existence, as if the job were part of my father's inheritance, I feel as if this white man has removed my intestines and splattered them out in the open for wild cats to feast on. But I didn't inherit the job: my father only left behind a valley and herds, not a job in America. Jobs in America belong to Blake and his white tribe, and losing one should never make me feel such excruciating pain, as if someone had died or I had lost a loved one.

War
Is what I know.
Beauty
Is what I carried in my belly.
Peace
Is what I expected you to teach me.
But
You place the pain of the black man in my belly,
And you have broken my spirit,
And keep my pocket dry,
And try to take my soul.
Words
Are my battle to bring you back.

I roll down the window and feel the air blowing in.

Something odd is crawling in my belly. I turn the radio on, but it does not help.

As I drive down the highway, the stark reality of it all strikes me with sudden force, as if I have been hit by a speeding car. My eyes itch. As I rub them with the palm of my hand, I feel moisture. Am I crying?

"That's impossible," I mutter to myself.

I have to find a way to suppress those goddamn tears. Somewhere I have heard that the Chinese character for the word *crisis* is composed of separate characters for *danger* and *opportunity*.

The danger of losing my job, and thus my sanity, is suddenly upon me. I have survived even greater perils in wartime. I know that somewhere in all this lies an opportunity I cannot see.

"Crisis is nothing but an opportunity riding in a dangerous wind," I chant to myself.

I repeat that Chinese proverb again and again. I know the power of words and their repetition. What else can I do to alter the hurt and despair I feel? What can I do? "Fuck that place," I cuss out loud. "I hope I never go back there."

When I cut off another driver and pass through a stop sign, I decide I had better slow down and pull over. I fetch my phone from my jacket and dial Latisha, an African American single mother and coworker.

She understands the situation.

"Hey, guess what?" I say.

"What?" she asks.

"They placed me on paid mandatory leave."

"I'm not surprised. But I am sorry. Are you surprised?"

"The suddenness of it all has shocked me a bit, but no, I'm not surprised. I guess I was an African before, but now this has turned me into an authentic black man."

"Welcome to the tribe. Now you know what we've been dealing with in this country for centuries."

"Whatever." I laugh. "I never denied being black, but really, I just have never had to deal with so much injustice in all my life."

American venom can torment and destroy the heart of a lion. At first I used to ignore the seemingly harmless white stares and random comments, but the assumption that my white colleagues were harmless soon turned into a nightmare. Now I can understand what made Deric break down and cry. But no, never, for as long as I live, will I allow myself to cry over another man's animosity, however destructive it may be. Still, it feels as if my heart is being ripped open and my identity slowly erased. However much I question why God has placed me in this predicament, I never question the certainty my father expressed lying on his deathbed: as his son, I shall own my words and never submit to someone my equal.

"Well, once again, welcome to America, black man."

"Thanks. I appreciate it."

28

LAWYER'S OFFICE.

"Good morning," the receptionist chirps. "How can I help you?"

"I want to file a discrimination complaint against my employer."

I can't wait to find someone to tell about my pain, this excruciating anguish, this rot in my soul. Now, finally, it's going to come out.

"Fill out these forms." She hands me a clipboard. "Do you have a pen?"

"Yes."

Holding the clipboard, I sit down.

Looking around the office for the first time, I notice that there are ten chairs, a printer, and four tiny cubicles. Conscious of the people entering the office, their faces, the color of their skin, their race, I become aware of the man sitting on my right, a black Latino. He has trouble speaking English. The man on my left is speaking Haitian Creole on his phone.

Three dark-skinned women sitting nearby seem to me to be African American. They are wearing cheap coats, shirts, and pants, and their shoes are frayed and worn. They sure are poor, I think.

Despite so many years working, here I am, huddling among the poorest and least educated. When you are a person of color, education doesn't necessarily advance your status. My income has been seized, my dignity diminished.

As I glance around, I can see no white people filling out forms—at least, not yet. Maybe poor whites will be coming in soon. Many of my white coworkers have never finished college. Although the company advises them repeatedly to return to school, they ignore such prompting. Yet they remain ensconced at the company, secure in their jobs.

As they climb that exclusive and still invisible employment ladder up and through the inner circles of white privilege, their defiance is rewarded.

I, on the other hand, during all those years, dutifully went back to school, earning my master's degree and a leadership certificate. Nevertheless, here I now sit, staring at these black faces as they crane their necks to steal a look in my direction.

In mute silence, they seem to know my story. They seem to know that my story is our story. Our glances are one. Our fears are one. Our poverty. Our declining health. Our dark humor against our internal hurt. The pain of bigotry has birthed us and brought us all to this place.

This is where I have ended up.

The elderly Haitian sitting next to me continues to stare. I return his gaze. "Good morning, sir."

"Good morning to you, my brother," he says in a hoarse voice.

Does he really mean to call me "brother" out of a feeling of kinship or because of our shared pain? I have never seen this man before, but here we find ourselves locked in the same piti-ful situation. He is indeed my brother.

"I have worked at the same job for seventeen years," he says to me in a heavy accent. I ponder the bridge of his thick glasses and the grease between his eyebrows. "But here I am now after all these years, getting fired."

"I know. I was at my job for many years before they let me go. Now, here I am too, just getting fired."

"Well, good luck to you, young man. I'll be praying for you."

"Thanks," I whisper.

I fill out the forms and hand them to the receptionist.

"Thank you," she says. "Just have a seat. Someone will be right with you."

On the wall opposite me is a poster of a black girl stand-ing above a collage of smiling children. Getting up and step-ping closer, I realize that the collage depicts children from all around the world just waking up to the bright, yellow sun of a new morning.

I begin to hear words lift up from the interior of my mind.

I watched my father die free
His nation of poets died with him
War carried me on its back
Here I walked in the land of Lincoln
I settled and made a life in the New England snow
My father died a free man
His freedom lived inside me
I saw his poem in the license plates of New Hampshire
Dad forgot to tell me the color of my skin
My father was born in the land of the nomads
I too was free until I held snow in my palm and felt its stink

*My legs are free, but their crooked white hands have shackled my
mind*

They pointed their crooked fingers at me

My father's freedom blocked their hands

I committed the crime of not seeing their white hands

My father believed I, his first son, was free

My father did not meet Lincoln

I met Lincoln in Team of Rivals, *and I knew what he looked
like*

I met the colored man, for America placed him inside of me

I am no longer my father's son, for he was free

America made me a black man.

*Her hands are unseen and untouched, but they are interwoven
with other hands*

*My freedom is in the hands of her crooked palms, for she is
America*

*What would my father say were I to tell him that I am not a
human*

That I am an African black body in America?

The secretary interrupts my reverie, calling me into the lawyer's office. She introduces me to a black woman lawyer. Her
high heels make her appear taller than she is. She is wearing a
well-tailored navy-blue suit and glasses with thick black frames.

Her office overlooks the Boston skyline. It is outfitted with
gray wooden chairs that look like antiques. A large shark hangs
from two thin wires above the portrait of a black-and-white
sailboat. A bookshelf and framed attorney credentials fill up
one wall. Her name is Thelma.

Thelma invites me in. I have been looking around for a black
lawyer to represent me, and I am elated to have found one.

She is darker than I am and must know a lot about my situation. America clearly has taught her the means to preserve her dignity.

"Nice office," I say. "I like how everything is so old."

"It's an old office."

"It even has that smell of old furniture." I grin.

"The chair you're sitting on dates from the 1930s."

"Wow, they last that long?" I ask her, no doubt with a surprised look, as I run my hands over the chair's leather.

"Yes," she says. "I bought them in 1989. They were very cheap back then, but just one of those chairs is now worth over a thousand dollars."

"Wow," I say. "I was living in Mogadishu when you bought those chairs."

Thelma leans back in her expensive chair. "Boyah, what can I help you with?"

"Well, I feel embarrassed to be talking to you about this, but I was fired from my job because of systematic discrimination. I had nothing but the shirt and shoes I was wearing when I arrived in this country, and when I got a job at this company, I was elated to join the American workforce."

"You're saying you were fired because of your race?"

I recount for her everything detailed in the emails I have sent for her to review, everything I have gone through. She is listening, and I want to trust her. Then again, somehow I can't. I sense from the way her words come out of her mouth that she doesn't think much of my story.

"I understand your point. But discrimination is very difficult to prove in court."

My neck itches. I place my hand over my mouth. My thoughts are spinning.

"Moreover, I haven't really done any discrimination cases for a long time," she goes on, locking her eyes on me. "To be completely honest with you, discrimination victims are mostly poor black people—and black people often don't have the money to pay for attorney fees. They have to pay with credit cards. In your case, it sounds like they simply don't want you there anymore."

"I understand," I say. "I don't want me there anymore either."

At that moment, my identity is fractured—neither African American nor Somali African. I am just a black man whose origins have been erased. Sleep has evaded me. Tears finally appear.

My words disconnect from me. And I talk about nothing but racism.

My world is now all about white people and nothing else.

"You're getting unemployment, right?"

"Yes. But I hate it. I want to work. I want to help people and do something."

"Are you saying you want your job back? Or are you open to some kind of a settlement? Maybe I can work out a settlement for you."

"Settlement? What kind of settlement?"

"Well," Thelma continues, "I could try to negotiate with the company and see if we could get them to agree to a year's pay as a settlement for your case."

"You could do that?"

"Yes. The settlement would come on top of your unemployment. But remember, I keep thirty percent of the settlement. Take your time, and think about it."

She's pushing the idea of a settlement, but my trust in her is beginning to fade. As she speaks, she reads through the email exchanges with Blake I sent her. She reads and reads and reads. Then she lifts up her head, staring directly into my eyes.

"To me, it doesn't look like there's much any lawyer can do to get you your job back."

"What are you trying to say?"

"From what I see in these emails from Blake and from what you have told me, they should have fired you a long time ago."

I am stunned. "So maybe you should be their lawyer."

"Don't misunderstand me," Thelma says. "They've got a lot of write-ups against you in your personnel file."

"You're telling me," I say. "You think all those emails about me put them in the right? Remember, I'm not the only one they wrote up. Every black employee there is going through the same kind of harassment."

"I'm focusing on your case. I'm your lawyer. I'm on your side, representing you."

"Right. That's the whole point. I'm paying you to represent me," I say. "But you're not really representing me the way I want you to represent me."

"The way I see it, you have two options. You can take them to court and try to sue to get your job back, or you can hire me to work for a settlement."

"I'm not so sure about that. Have you done anything to dig deeper and look into my story?"

"What do you mean?" she says.

"Your words tell me that you don't really care about my situation," I say.

"No, I do care. But I'm giving you my professional opinion and letting you know that I think you have only two options in this situation. You can sue and try to get your job back.

Setting aside who's right and wrong, it's clear they really don't want you there. So, in my view, if you do succeed and return to work, you'll end up getting fired again."

"How do you know that? Even if I do my best and perform well at my job?"

"Yes," she says. "It is easy for them to find something to use to terminate you. Or you can try to negotiate a settlement."

"Okay," I say.

"Let me speak frankly. I'm not the person to help you." Looking at her, I keep watching her face while listening to her words. I was so sure that she could help me. "Yes, I may be black, but I haven't been through the same experiences you have."

"Okay," I mutter, shaking my head.

"I was born in a white suburban city. I grew up with white people," she continues. "All my friends are white. My husband is white."

"I understand," I say. "But I wanted a black lawyer to represent me."

"I'm not the lawyer you're looking for. I'm sorry."

"I understand you," I say. "But I just got fired from my job because of my race."

It feels like she's telling me she's white too.

"Look," she says, "you aren't from this country. Being black is a terrible predicament here in America."

She sees the open bewilderment on my face at her matter-of-fact comment. "I may not have been born in this country," I tell her, "but I have lived in America far longer than the time I spent in Africa."

"I'm trying to be frank with you, Boyah. To survive you must cultivate peace of mind when it comes to the racial situation in America."

"For over ten years," I said, "I really tried my best to cultivate my peace of mind. But they just would not leave me alone."

"Who are 'they'?"

"Who else?" I say. "White people at my job. They picked at me and picked at me to the point of madness, until in the end they fired me."

"Listen. I have my law practice," she says. "I do well for my clients. I do not spend any time thinking about being black or the black problems in this country. I look black to you, but I consider myself American. I could even say I may be a little racist myself against black people because I was raised that way. And I constantly have to check myself to make sure that I am not acting out those feelings."

Her statement is so truthful, and yet so hurtful, I will remember it forever.

You cannot live without following someone. Say you are born on a bright day to a human family, but your parents leave you behind with a family of monkeys.

As you are growing up, you eat with the monkeys. You play with the monkeys. You giggle with them. You climb mountains and jump between the branches of trees. You learn the language of monkeys. And then sometime later, you rejoin your human family. You look like any other human, but your language, your rituals—everything else about you—belongs to the monkeys.

In what she says lies a hidden but inescapable truth.

She has been raised by white monkeys.

The image of a black woman that Thelma sees reflected in the mirror each day differs from the image she sees of herself. Her peace of mind supersedes everything else, and in her mind, she creates an alternative living space where she escapes

America's rejection of blacks as a whole and Trump's brutality and the murders of Breonna Taylor and Ahmaud Arbery and George Floyd.

I am nevertheless shocked by how she sees herself. However, I do understand her need for acceptance and safety, for money and survival.

I smile because I respect Thelma's honesty. I have the utmost respect for her as a human being—with flaws, but my equal.

"Maybe you can teach me something I don't know about all this," I say. "How is it that America looks at you as just another American and not as a black person?"

"What do you mean?" she asks. "You're a naturalized American now, right?"

"Yes, I am. When I came to this country as a teenager almost thirty-three years ago, I did not know much about the importance of skin color."

"What changed in you?"

"Nothing changed in me. America made me a black man."

"I am not sure where," she says, "but I read a report that says black women have an easier time dealing with American racism than black men. You certainly are acting like a black man now, it seems to me." She smiles, sipping her coffee.

"You consider yourself a black woman?"

"Isn't it obvious?" she says. "Yes, I am a black woman, but besides the color of my skin, there is nothing in my life that would be considered black."

Her words touch a nerve in my mind. I shake my head. I appreciate her honesty, but I am frustrated I can't do anything about how wrong she is. "As you said," I tell her, "you're black. You're a lawyer. You're married to a white man. You have white friends. Your reality protects you from America's lethal treatment of black people."

"If you are going to live here," she says, "you will need to find that part of America where you can find peace of mind."

"I like your honesty," I say. "Being black in America is a constant and unending battle."

"Where are you from, exactly?"

"Somalia."

"Oh," she says. "I'm sorry."

"What are you sorry about?"

"Somalia is going through war right now, isn't it?"

"Yes, it is, but things are calmed down now. Trust me when I tell you I'd rather go through war than put up with American prejudice."

"Maybe," she says. "So you went through the war?"

"Yes," I say. "I have seen it all, and I never thought that I would ever compare it to anything else. War is temporary, but the pain caused by racism is passed down. Black children inherit that pain the way white children inherit property or trust funds." The pain I endure now, my children will inherit.

"I never really thought about it the way you are breaking it down for me now. You might not realize it, but you have an advantage not being born in America."

"What advantage?" I say. "I am educated, just like all the other black people working at that company, yet America looks at me and treats me as nothing more than a black body."

"That, precisely, is the point. My body might be black, but I do not consider myself black. I feel free."

"Maybe," I say, "you can teach me how to escape from America."

"You do have that option, don't you?"

"I don't understand. Tell me."

"You can consider going back to your country," Thelma says. "Or you can drop the race-baiting black victimhood mentality and get along and go to work."

"Race-baiting black victimhood mentality," I repeat slowly. "You really don't understand, do you? This saga has affected my peace of mind, and I can't sleep anymore. I'm financially and emotionally wrecked."

"Look," she says with a sigh. "I need to get back to work."

29

ONE DAY SOON AFTER I SEE THE LAWYER, I DRIVE TO MY FAVOR-
ite Starbucks in Medford.

I grab a tall dark roast coffee and amble toward my favorite spot, facing the large picture window, where I usually sit and look out at the snowbanks, the traffic lights, the moving vehicles, the police cruisers with their sirens blaring, and everything beyond.

Oh, no, the seat is taken!

A large white man wearing glasses is sitting in my favorite seat.

I take another seat nearby and, sipping my coffee, simply watch him. His hair is wild. His beard is pointy. His nose is large. His overgrown mustache covers his upper lip. Clearly, his mind is engrossed in the large book he's reading.

After a few moments, I get up and go over to him.

"Excuse me," I say, standing over him. He looks up. "I'm sorry for interrupting you."

"Sure. What is it?"

"My name is Boyah," I mention. "I'm a writer." I am in pursuit of freedom.

"That's nice," he says, somewhat bewildered.

He pulls his glasses down to the bridge of his nose. His eyebrows lift up a bit.

"You happen to be sitting in my favorite seat. If you wouldn't mind giving up the seat for me, I'd be happy to buy you whatever you want."

"Oh, no, no, no," he says, as if embarrassed by my offer. "You can have it. I'm just about to leave anyway." He begins to collect his things. "Good luck with your writing."

"Thank you so much," I reply as my stomach softens a bit.

I find myself associating his whiteness with the turmoil roiling in my belly. I hope to survive, but I know that the ultimate therapy will come from the ink of my pen.

"That's really kind of you," I say.

"I'm not a writer myself," he says, collecting his books and papers into his briefcase. "But I really admire people who write. Have you published anything?"

"Sure. Some pieces. You can google my name. Boyah J. Farah." I say it proudly, like an accomplished writer.

"That's a fine name." He smiles as he stops to type my name into his phone. "Does Boyah mean anything?"

"It means 'great writer'?" I tease him. "No, just kidding. For me, 'Boyah' has personal significance: it means 'African'; it means 'American'; it means 'black man living in America.' But then, I am more than that: I am a human being just like you."

He shakes my hand and tells me he teaches law nearby. At that, a light goes on in my mind.

"Are you a practicing lawyer?"

"Technically, I'm retired. But I teach part-time."

I put my backpack beneath the table and sit down opposite him.

"I have to tell you, I'm looking for a good lawyer," I confess.

"Is that so? What kind of attorney are you looking for?"

"I lost my job."

"Lost your job? That's too bad. What happened?"

"Well, I got fired because I'm black."

"I'm really sorry to hear that. Unfortunately, I think that kind of thing is probably all too common. I think I know someone who may be able to help." He looks down at his phone again, scrolling through names. "She's a great lawyer and a friend of mine, and she's passionate about the plight of black people in this country."

"Is she black?"

"No. But she's decent and fair."

"Mmmmm," I whisper.

"Do you prefer a black lawyer?"

"Oh, no. No, no."

But the truth is I feel a bit embarrassed by my overt suspicion of "white" lawyers. With the words of Thelma still echoing in my mind, I am a bit confused and unsure. How am I supposed to navigate the terrible complexity of America's warring black and white tribes? I find myself unsure now about black lawyers too.

I know that my skin is black and that I am African, but I am hurt. When I look at America and only see warring black tribes and warring white tribes, I feel trapped like a bird in a cage. America has damaged me that way. But I still want to believe in the goodness of humanity.

"All I want is a good lawyer who can understand my situation and represent me fairly."

"Hanna is a good lawyer. She has a proven record, and many clients who say good things about her."

"That's great. I really appreciate your help," I say, looking him directly in his eyes.

Before my father left me and departed to the land of the dead, he always used to tell me to look people in the eyes when I speak with them.

Looking directly in someone's eyes projects strength with confidence.

"Here," he says, showing me the screen of his phone. "Here's her contact information."

"I'm going to call her right now. I really need her services."

"Right. Give her a call," he tells me as he finishes packing his briefcase and stands up to leave. "So, I guess you come here quite a bit."

"I do. And every time I come here, I sit in this seat. And I write as if I'm in love."

"That's great. I'm really glad to meet you. And I will definitely read your work."

"I appreciate that. People like you make me believe in the goodness of humanity."

America has cracked me open like a dropped egg.

Things were not good, and I couldn't have felt more despondent than when I first entered Starbucks. I felt betrayed and abandoned by both white and black people. But now, here I am sitting and chatting with an elderly white man whom I have just met, and he is not only helping me, but telling me how much he likes my writing. My soul needs his uplifting comments the way a tree needs water and sunshine. Unfortunately, that is not enough to heal the hurt inside. He turns and walks out, as rain begins to beat down outside. He pulls his jacket over his head and runs to the car.

As he jumps into his car and begins to back out, I dial

Hanna's office. When I get through, I tell her who gave me her name.

"He's a friend of mine. How can I help you?"

"I'm looking for legal representation in an employee discrimination case."

"Yes, I may be able to help. I charge three hundred dollars an hour, but the initial consultation is free."

"That's pretty expensive. But I need the help."

"Would you like to come in and discuss it?"

"Do you have time available tomorrow?"

I hear the clicking of her computer as she types. My fingers begin to shake on their own. My stomach gurgles, and I feel that something is moving inside, but I have not dropped a stool for a week. And so I am hopeful that that soft stool is pushing down.

"How about nine tomorrow morning?" she says.

"Sure."

"Please text me your email," she says, "and I'll send you a confirmation."

"Will do. See you tomorrow."

As she hangs up the phone, I rush to the bathroom, pull my pants down, and sit on the toilet. My stomach is gurgling as if I'm sick. I hold my breath, tighten my stomach, and push out. Nothing. I should go back and see the doctor again, I think. But what would I say?

I'm not exactly sick, but then again, I am. I'm not feeling any physical pain, but then again, everything hurts. I no longer take showers. My armpits smell. My back teeth hurt.

My hair is wild, like the hair of someone who has gone mad. Something beneath my skin is itching. None of those pathologies belong to me. They belong to America.

I have nothing but my urge to write.

Pulling my pants up, I step out of the bathroom and go back to my favorite seat and sit leaning my head against the wall and looking out the window, watching everything: the moving cars and trucks and random people running in the rain.

Much greater than the immediate world I'm looking at is the world that occupies my mind. All my symptoms—my indisposition and infirmity, my fragility—point to the evil magic of America's power over the lives of black bodies living in America.

Like the power exerted by talismans and amulets in rural Africa, America's man-made laws and customs are designed to instill fear, break the spirit within, and make me drop to my knees. I cannot become what America wants me to be, however, because I cannot and will not betray the legacy of my father. I must stand up and live free until my own soul departs into the land of the dead.

Nevertheless, my body is upset. My soul is bitter. My tongue is dry. My eyes are twitching. I yearn to walk alone in the rain with my mouth open and my tongue lapping the raindrops, without the thought of America upsetting my mind. Yet that childhood reservoir of love for America is not completely dry.

That old man lying in my soul, my departed father, is someone I cannot betray.

When I start to get a headache, I begin to write.

Dear America,

I came to your land so that you could help me restore what war had broken within me. I was humbled by war, for I am a simple man whose desires are insignificant.

I like dark roast coffee. I like to walk in the park. I like sitting at the beach. I like looking at the stars in the moonless sky. I like comfortable chairs. I like looking at your trimmed grass. And occasionally, I like driving on your American highways. When I first stepped onto your soil, I was neither black nor white. But you turned me into a disposable black body living on your soil. Understand, however, that ultimately it is my decision alone whether to accept the disgraceful, demeaning position to which you assign me. In the land of my forefathers, I was born free: life lived under oppression was never part of my family history. Today, I continue to inhabit my father's words, uttered to me so long ago, and I live free. I will die free. I write to you not to understand myself, but so that you can comprehend and master yourself. I am one of your sons, a counterforce to your oppression, a simple healer of the living, and one who dwells on and awaits death unblinking. My experiences in life are not provincial or small-souled. My nomadic life in the Nugaal Valley formed me to view life as something immense and infinite. In war I have seen the heart-wrenching execution of an innocent bystander and been touched by the kindness of a stranger sharing with me in my need his last bit of food and water.

America, I believe in your goodness, but I also know your capacity for evil, written in the blood of your enslaved children. The police belong to you. The financial system belongs to you. The media belongs to you. But my mind belongs to me alone, and so does my body. You have weakened both, but my pen belongs to me and shall not rest until my soul glides through the different galaxies like

a soaring bird. Through my singing lips, hope springs:
and the gaze of my eyes, the smile of my cheeks, and the
rhythm of my body all belong to me.

My mind is spinning, and I make myself stop typing.

I place my laptop into my backpack, zip it shut, and turn
to walk out into the rain. Just outside the door, an old white
woman with broken front teeth extends her hand, asking for
change. Wearing dirty black pants, a white shirt, and a ripped
bright red jacket, she has been there all along, but I had not
paid her any attention. I am struck because I usually take
notice of homeless panhandlers and acknowledge them with a
greeting, a simple smile, or whatever change I can give them.
When we were on the run during the war, my mother always
impressed upon us the notion that God favors the weak in
society.

Smiling, she extends her cup as I pass through the door.

"Can I ask you something?" I say after I drop some change
into her cup.

"Certainly, my dear."

"Do you pray?"

"Absolutely. I never lay my body down for the night without
first praying to God."

Judging from her diction, it seems this homeless woman
with her wide dimples and striking face is educated. Her body
may have been wrinkled, but her beauty remains intact.

"Right now, I am facing some troubles," I say to her. "Would
you pray for me?"

"Certainly. I will definitely pray for you, my child. And God
will bless you."

The paleness of her skin is noticeable, and I question myself for a moment. Doesn't this woman belong to the tribe of my oppressor?

But then again, I blame my conditioning in America for training me to notice the pigmentation of this woman's skin. We belong to the same species, and she is, like me, a human being. I find that I care for her. And she is praying for me, so she must care for me too.

After her prayers, I feel at ease, and the following morning, I wake up and pray for a successful day.

I feel uplifted by the thought that I am going to benefit from the prayers of that elderly white homeless woman panhandling in front of Starbucks. I put on a black suit, grab a coffee, and hop on the highway. Pulling up to the lawyer's office, I park the car and walk into the high-rise building. Standing just inside the door, I stop to contemplate the building atrium and the sun shooting in from its golden ceiling. Tree plantings surround a waterfall cascading down the wall, and a restaurant sits on the street level with a mostly white clientele.

I walk over to the concierge desk and ask for a pass to the fourteenth floor.

I take the elevator and arrive at the lawyer's office. I marvel at the decor: the huge picture windows, the modern art covering the walls, the flat-screen television tuned in to CNN, the spherical chandelier dropping down from the ceiling.

The receptionist, a white woman, is wearing high heels and a glittering Rolex watch. I tell her I'm here to see my attorney, and I give the receptionist her name.

"Have a seat, sir. She's expecting you. I'll call her for you."

I take a seat and pull out Ta-Nehisi Coates's *Between the World and Me*.

After a few minutes, I hear my name. "Boyah?"

I look up to see a white woman dressed in a suit. She must be Hanna. She extends her hand to me in greeting and motions for me to follow her.

"Welcome, Boyah. Let's go into my office."

As I stand to follow her, I realize how tall she is. She leads me into a conference room. We both sit down. My thoughts are running wild. She is tall and white, but I must try to trust her. Still, I have my doubts that she can represent me honestly.

Then again, something else reminds me that it is not possible for all white people to be bigoted. Besides, I'm the one who's going to be paying her.

Maybe I should ask for a discount?

She walks me through my options and explains how much pursuing my case might cost, both in money and mental energy.

Here I am, down-and-out and flat broke. But I agree to the fees and sign.

Some days later, I am sitting in my favorite seat at Starbucks again, and my phone rings. When I pick up, it is Hanna.

"Boyah, do you have time to come by my office either later today or tomorrow?"

"I can come right now."

"Great. I'll see you at three this afternoon."

"Wonderful. Do you have good news for me?"

"Yes. They've made an offer to settle."

"Really? Should I begin driving to your office now?"

"I'm going to the office once I leave the courthouse," she says. "I'll see you at three."

That afternoon, by the time I drive over and make my way up to her office, Hanna is already there waiting for me in the conference room.

We greet each other and sit.

"Look," she says. "I do have good news for you, but it is up to you to accept or decline."

"Sure. What have you got? Tell me."

Eagerly, I watch her lips to see what words will come from her mouth.

She is composed with her tongue.

"Tell me," I repeat.

"For you to walk away, the company is willing to offer you two years' salary to settle your complaint."

At that moment, the hurt and betrayal surges. I hate my job. I hate Boston. I hate America. I hate white people. I hate myself. I feel lost. I want the return of my internal peace.

I cannot fight. I will not fight. I am done.

"But," she continues, "you only have until tomorrow to decide if you accept or not."

If I accept their offer, I will not have a chance to prove my case, but I will be able to move on from this nightmare. If I reject their offer, they could prolong the case until my health and savings are totally depleted.

"Hold on just a minute. I'll be right back. I've got to use the restroom."

"The bathroom is just over there."

I go in. Standing inside and looking at myself in the mirror, the posture of my body gawking back at me, I seem like something broken. I don't recognize myself in the body I see in the mirror. The ovals of my eyes are red, and the bags under my eyes are thick. My cheeks are hollowed out. My face is bony and thin. Tufts of hair stick out from my uncombed head.

I can't say right then that I hate myself, but I also do not really like what I see. I must accept who I am now, acknowledge my situation and move on. My mother was right when she used to say to me that whatever is happening now is a thousand years older than I am.

I leave the restroom and return to the conference room, where Hanna is still sitting and waiting.

As I sit down again, I tell her, "I don't have to wait until tomorrow. I'll take the deal right now."

Before I leave the office, I sign all the paperwork she needs.

As I get back in my car and head home, I realize how much I have wanted to run away and escape. As I drive, what begins to beat through my mind like African drums is another afternoon a long time ago. I am living with my *ayeyo* in the Nugaal Valley. The yellow sun is falling and showering the valley below with its rays. Walking behind our grazing herds, I carry a carved wooden cup half filled with tea in one hand and a stick for tending our goats and sheep in the other.

Sitting down on an anthill, I can survey the entire valley with a glance. Up above, just below the clouds, I notice an eagle leisurely soaring through the sky, its eyes gazing on everything below.

My eyes are following the eagle carefully when suddenly I see him dive and strike his claws into the back of a large deer. Surprised by the assault, the deer flees and bucks as the razor-sharp claws sink into its back and tighten their grip. Struggling and lurching forward, the deer struggles and jerks hard to escape into the safety of the trees.

After some time the deer, seemingly resigned to its fate, collapses, but continues to writhe violently as the bird claws and slashes and rips open its back. Blood spurts out, and the doomed deer, in its death throes, seems to accept the inevitable and succumb.

30

WITH THE SEVERANCE MONEY, I BOOK PASSAGE FOR ME AND
Mama to return to the Nugaal Valley in northern Somalia, the
land of my birth and inheritance, the land of my father and
forefathers. As we arrive at the airport, it is six o'clock in the
morning, and the streetlights are still on. The sun hidden behind Boston's skyscrapers is attempting to replace the dark-
ness of the night. It is January cold, and it is expected to snow.
Wearing a red headwrap with black stripes and a black face
mask, Mama is pushing a cart with her two suitcases as she
walks through Terminal E at Boston Logan Airport.

"You look great, Mama," I say. Now that my siblings are
grown and have an education and jobs and families of their
own, Mama is free to retire to Somalia. And I am happy that
the old man in the grave, my father, is pleased that I completed
my education and turned around to help as many people as I
could. I still wonder if he knows that I am fighting to restore
my identity in the land of Obama and Trump. Still burning in
my mind is the wildfire of that troubled Somalia where civil
war raged, and I never thought I would be running back there.
But I find that I can't accommodate the sneaky sharp sting of
racism in America—it makes me sick and sleepless and pushes

me to keep running. Despite all the troubles of my life in America, I remain an optimist. In Somalia, I think, I can bring about real change. I can teach and build a school. I can build a hospital. I can farm. If I survived catastrophic loss, I can do anything. I am charged with energy to build up and to work for the good of humanity. But now we are running from the sting of the snow, from the weight of the white man's prejudice, toward the freedom of the Nugaal Valley, toward restoration.

"You look great, Mama," I repeat. She does not reply but keeps gliding along stylishly, moving one foot after the other as if she has missed using her legs. The diabetic shoes on her feet are helping her walk, or perhaps her legs are urging her body to hit the road. She has spent over a year in isolation due to COVID-19, and I am beyond elated for her that she has made it out, that we are on the move again. Isn't life all about being in motion, whether you are on a bicycle, in a car, or on a plane?

My mother and I have been running together all our lives, striving to reach out and break loose from the trap of doom and death destined for us. We ran when the civil war began in Somalia thirty years ago. We ran through the malevolent jungle swarming with deadly animals. We ran from one rotten refugee camp to another. We ran through the falling snow of America's suburban landscape, aliens, widowed and orphaned, with nothing to call our own.

"Mama, slow down," I say, trudging behind her. "You're walking too fast."

"Boy, make use of those legs. You better keep up," she says. I am glad Mama is making jokes, but her life has been an ongoing attempt to escape pain and loss. In her thirties, she buried her beloved husband—the tall man with deep dimples and Afro hair—and life as a widowed war refugee followed. In raising us and bringing us through, she buried her own vitality, just as I buried the better part of my life in America as a black man. She buried most of her close friends. And she buried her country. Now, in 2021, Mama and I are still running—better to keep running than to fall asleep in America, cowering in fear.

Mama, however, does not continue to carry in her spirit any of that pain and grief and loss. Rather, those experiences have made her resilient, an eyewitness to tragedy who is still smiling. And what about me? She hasn't been exposed to the rejection of America that made me into a black man, into Boyah J. Farah, the writer who believes that life is not to be endured, but to be seized in the art of literature.

Coming to the airport ticket counter and looking around at that sea of passengers, waiting and talking and pulling their suitcases, my eyes are looking for black faces. An Indian couple are standing in the corner. A headscarf-wearing Middle Eastern woman with her five children is sleeping on a seat near the counter. A short, muscular black man is pushing a three-wheeled gray trash can. He sings in whispering tones to himself, as if he has accepted his fate in America. And then there is that white state trooper in his best blue uniform, wearing Ray-Ban aviator sunglasses as he stands at the corner, looking as if he is observing us—or then again, maybe he isn't. A man and his girlfriend are standing in line and speaking a foreign language, holding hands and looking into each other's eyes, as if in love. There is nothing on earth more moving or more beautiful than love in its inception, a mystery, like life, not to be mastered but rather tolerated.

"You're just too slow," Mama repeats, still teasing me.

"Mama," I say. "You're really happy we're going back, aren't you?"

"Yes," she replies. I can hear her smile, her lips concealed behind a mask.

When I first arrived in America, I really thought that my life was changed forever and that I could make my life as restful and constant as America's green grass. But now, as I run behind Mama through the airport, this is not how I envisioned my life would turn out. The hurt is unbearable. I want to pick up a poster, write "Black Lives Matter," and stand near Boston Common holding the sign up, facing the road and shouting so that drivers and pedestrians can see and hear me. But such is not in me. So then, what can I do? Should I sing and dance or should I fly? Sometimes I even wish I could pick up a gun like my father to fight and die. He believed in the power of the gun to bring about change, but I belong to the written word. I wish I could fly.

As we check in our suitcases, I ask, "Mama, remember when we landed for the first time at this airport?" Back then, when we saw escalators for the first time, none of us dared step onto the moving plates. I stood watching the Americans effortlessly step onto that novel mechanism, and fearlessly placed my foot on the first step, but suddenly lost my bravery and pulled back. As we struggled to figure out how to ride that strange moving machine, I remember a photographer taking pictures of our bewilderment: eventually we figured it out and learned to climb onto the escalator like other Americans.

"Yes, that was many years ago. But in America we have learned how to live." The floor is shiny, clean and beautiful as the rays of the morning sun slip through the large glass windows of the airport. Mama is cheerful and relieved. The morning sky is beginning to release snow.

"Yes, that's true," I say. "But I am so glad to be leaving here and going back to Africa with you." As I assimilated the beauty of America and made English my own, I savored the taste of pizza and pasta with meatballs. I learned to walk on that green grass and experienced the freedom of driving the highways of America. Holding snow in the palm of my hand, I found out how to live with the threat of winter always coming, with police and coworkers aiming for my destruction. America has seized me, and I am running to free myself from its weight.

"Mama, did you ever think that you would return to Somalia?" I ask.

"Yes, of course." She smiles, looking at me. As we stand in a long TSA line with our carry-on bags still on the cart, she adjusts her face mask and murmurs something behind her lips, as if she does not want me to hear. "I belong over there," she chirps. After a lifetime of hurt, she still carries on with a smile and a joke on her lips. Her hope never seems to diminish.

"No, Mama," I react. "We both belong over there."

"But you came to America as a young boy," she says. "And although you have seen a lot of trouble here in America, this country still belongs to you."

"No," I correct her. "This country belongs to Donald Trump and his white tribe. White people are the majority, and what they are doing to black people is really wrong."

"Yes, that may be true," Mama responds. "And it even appears to be getting worse. But really, aren't you tired of talking about Trump all the time?"

It is January 2021, and Mama has been listening to what Trump is saying. She knows from experience that such words from his mouth can inspire others to kill. Mama just wants to live in peace, to sit in her reclining chair and sip tea.

"Yes, I really am tired of talking about him," I respond. "But

Trump is all over the news. There's nothing else to watch." The America that I know is now out in the open for all to see, and Trump is revealing the America that I and black people experience every day. Some may deny its existence, but Trump's America is the legacy he inherited from his forefathers.

"I think Americans are tired of him," she says. "I'm tired of him. He's destroyed America. He reminds me of the warlords who destroyed Somalia."

"Really?"

"He uses tribal rhetoric, social grievance, and mindless religion to divide Americans from one another. That's what happened in Somalia. Once the country is divided against itself, it's hard to put it back together." Trump understands how to exploit fear in politics, and he uses his charisma and popularity to aggravate the feelings white Americans have about becoming a minority and losing their country. His language is awakening their brutality, and he rode that cruel heartlessness right up into the White House. But history has a way of catching up to you, so now Americans are reacting violently across the country, whether it is Black Lives Matter demanding the removal of monuments of confederate generals like Robert E. Lee, or Proud Boys storming the Capitol building. Trump's words are sharp and filthy and riddled with lies. I know where his words are heading; they're leading America into the land of the dead. Trump is taking his own life—and the life of America—into a dark hole, into a place of broken despair and myopic hopelessness. One day, perhaps, the mothers of America may find themselves burying the corpses of their own children in shallow graves.

"Trump cannot escape the destiny his words inspire," Mama remarks.

"I think you're right." What else can I do but agree? Her resilience is unmatched. Her hope is unbroken, her words prophetic.

"But in the end, he lost the election, didn't he?" Mama reminds me. "And Biden appears to me a decent man. I pray and hope for the best from Biden." Her devotion to America is inspired by her escape through that deadly forest. Her love for America, like her love for children, is raw and unquestionable. I too love America, but I want America to reciprocate.

"As I was saying, you belong to this country in a way that I do not," Mama says. "And you will always be different. I have always been fearful for you because of that." But my attachment to America is more chaotic than hers. All the most important milestones of my adult life have occurred in America. High school. Learning to drive. Finishing college. Working. And as I began to know myself as a black man in America, my love affair with America shattered. Cursing cops. George Floyd. Deric. I have been dancing with a deadly rattlesnake; the sickness in me belongs to America. But I didn't survive war just so I could become white America's plaything. I am determined to endure, and my words must whip your ears to listen before your green trimmed grass withers away and turns into drifting dust. When I arrived in America, I never thought I would return to Somalia. Do I belong here? Do I belong there? Do I belong anywhere?

"You say I'm something different?" I repeat after her. "I'm trying to understand."

"You spent thirty years and most of your childhood in this country. You can't just discard all that and throw it away. The way you view the world, the way you think and act, everything about you belongs to this country," she says. "You may as well say this is your country. You just need to get away for a while and turn your hurt into something meaningful and productive." The wisdom of her words is as real as the rays of the lifting sun. I take a few steps forward as the line moves up a bit, but my ears belong to her.

"I just feel like my whole life has been a mistake."

"You are not a mistake," Mama says. "You belong to us." Mama speaks from a place of intelligence, and I wish I had the wisdom and patience to listen to her. I ask God sitting in the clouds to grant me the wisdom not only to listen to her but to break down her words and bring them to life. "America may be your country, but it is not your only country. You belong to the land of your father in Africa."

"Yes, that's true," I say. "I am an African, but I am also an American."

Still, I wonder whether I made a mistake. My feelings do not belong to me anymore: they are detached and foreign. As Mama speaks her words to me, from somewhere deep inside me a spirit of melancholy arises. Am I wrong to insist on my dignity? Am I overreacting? Have I forgotten that I am my father's son? Or have I lost who I am? I am much too free to be what America wants me to be. I am still that boy sitting on an anthill, watching over the valley. I am a fallen leaf drifting through the air. I am the wind. Inside of me, my grief and torment in America is clashing with the nomadic warrior, the part of me that grew up running free in the Nugaal Valley, the side of me I inherited from my departed father.

"I have been on the move for so many years," I say. "When am I going to settle down with a real sense of ownership? Was it a mistake to feel ownership in America?"

"Ownership?" she murmurs. "In this life, you may sometimes feel that you own something, but in the end, you never really own anything. One day, we all die."

"I know we all die," I reply. "But America is constantly reminding me that my vitality is in their hands and that I do not belong."

"You may feel that way," she says. "But when we were running away from war and death, America was the only country that opened its door for you."

We go through TSA and walk toward the plane, but thoughts are spinning through my mind. Mama and I board and sit next to each other.

"I mean, as an educated adult, don't you think you have choices?" Mama asks.

"Certainly I do," I retort. "When we first arrived, I never conceived of a life outside of America. But America has kept reminding me that I am a black man on its soil, a nothing. Her original sin has trapped me, and I am having trouble thinking of myself outside that American narrative. But, yes, I think I do have choices."

"My son," Mama says with a strong motherly voice. As my ears capture her words, I smile because she hardly ever uses those words. *My son.* Maybe she is about to tell me something serious. "How can you feel trapped?"

"I have been feeling trapped for some time. All my black American friends feel the same."

"But you are a writer, aren't you?" Mama has seen me sitting and enduring long hours of writing. As a Somali, she admires poets and singers and anyone who uses words to connect with humanity and create something worthy. "Writers never feel trapped. They release their hurt onto pages. You can do the same. Trust me, you can write about your hurting in America."

"I used to write a lot about our lives during the war and in the refugee camps," I tell her. "That writing helped me escape the carnage I witnessed during the war and find meaning."

"Yes, that was good . . . ," she whispers, glancing at me, waiting for me to say more.

"But I write about America now. And about how America made me a black man."

"Yes, that's a good thing. But never forget, you are an African who has spent thirty years living in America. You are different, and your perspective is critical. America needs to hear you."

She sits immobile as her eyes descend into sleep. As I sit next to her, her words spin inside of me. I watch the snow falling and covering America through the window. As the plane lifts, my view of America shrinks until I can see it no more. Now there is distance, something I need so my writing can grapple with my America.

I attempt to close my eyes, but my mind will not stop ruminating. I put on headphones and search the airplane's music channel for something sleep-inducing. In frustration, I force my eyes to close and keep them shut for a while, but nothing stops my mind from spinning. My thoughts are running wild. I am sick.

The plane vibrates as it cuts through thick clouds, and I open my eyes to consider the figure of Mama sitting beside me. She removes her mask, and I see a host of wrinkles scattered on her face. Some of those wrinkles on her face are new. Her wrinkles are a reminder of her coming death, the final chapter of her life in the land of the living. Her spirit is one with her body, but her body of work, her legacy, remains with me. Death is everywhere now. And as I consider the figure of Mama aging and flying in the direction of death, my thoughts turn to the memory of my father's last day, my last day with him, the day I watched him gasp for air until he was no more.

It is Monday, July 24, 1989. I am eleven years old, and we are four sons and three daughters—our fourth sister is married and living in the United States. With Mama and Dad, we are all living in a modest compound of three detached rooms, an open-sky bathroom, and a stand-alone kitchen. Mama is in her thirties. Her silky brown skin is smooth against the light of the lifting sun. Her teeth are white. Her eyes are clear as a baby's eyes. Like other women of her generation with their long hair, Mama's long hair reaches below her butt. Through my bedroom window, I see Mama wearing a dress with red, yellow, and blue patterns. The slow morning air is flooding her hair. And then I stand on my bed and put my head out of the window and look up and over the yellow morning of Mogadishu's rising sun. Several *cock-a-doodle-doos*, mingling with other low- and high-pitched sounds from the neighborhood roosters, cut through the calm air.

"Where's your father?" Mama asks me as she stands with Luqman, my youngest brother, wrapped around her waist.

"In the bathroom," I answer from inside my room. The Mogadishu sky is clearing up from the faint shadow of the sun still emerging from its hole in the distance. The heat is making my armpits sweat. God refuses the rain, and the grasses around me are lifeless, dry and brown. The branches of our tree are leafless. The soil is dry. On the left side of the house, two dead butterflies are decaying in our tiny garden, and beneath the butterflies the soil is thirsty. This morning, the earth smells of decay.

"He didn't sleep last night," I hear her mutter.

Stepping outside, I respond, "I think Dad isn't doing too well."

"Stay with him," Mama says to me, reminding me that it was my filial duty. I look at her walk back into her room and close the door behind her. Then I lift my eyes to gaze at the bright cloud formations, like a ruptured belly hanging in the sky.

"Argh," I hear coming from the bathroom. At first, I do not react. But when I hear "Aww" from Dad again, I rise, take a few steps, grab Dad's toothbrush, and stand at the bathroom door. I pick up his T-shirt from the ground and sling it around my neck. I love how the T-shirt holds the aroma of Dad's body odor with aftershave. When Dad pulls his shorts down and sits on the toilet, I abruptly walk out of the bathroom and sit down in the sand for a moment.

As Dad lingers in the bathroom, I return to my room and lie in my bed. After a few minutes, I hear Dad walk out of the bathroom and sit in the courtyard.

"Come here!" he groans out to me.

I walk out of my room and amble over to where he is sitting in the courtyard on a low, four-legged chair covered by red, white, and black animal skins. I sit cross-legged in the sand, watching his lips.

"You are my son," Dad says in a hoarse voice, turning his head with his bushy beard and pointy mustache first toward the sky and then toward me.

"Do you understand what I'm telling you?" Dad demands forcefully.

I don't understand what he is trying to tell me, so I keep looking at his mouth and the way he moves his cane in the sand. Digging my fingers beneath the soft sand, I can feel the cool moisture penetrating upward through my fingers to the palm of my hand. When Dad notices that I am a bit confused, he speaks: "God planted us in this harsh land of Somalia. My mother died when I was two, so I grew up without a mother."

"I never knew that." I sigh.

"Then in my teens my father got ill, so I faithfully took care of him until he died." He pauses, his breathing labored.

"My father was the tallest man in the city," he points out.

"So that's how you got to be so tall," I observe, nodding to urge him to say more.

"But he was not even fifty when he died, and we buried his body there in the coastal city of Eyl, where we lived."

"Did you ever visit the place where he was buried?"

"Yes, I remember him. When I was healthy, I used to sit at his gravesite and pray for him. Then I moved to Mogadishu and met your mother. When we had you, it was the happiest day of our lives. You were my first son. Living your life is like putting your hand into the lair of a snake, but I expect you to overcome." He grabs his cane and draws a shape like a mountain picture in the sand.

"Oh." I still don't know how to reply. Dad never talks to me about his family. Moisture gathers in his eyes, and he clears his throat against the soft emotions. He coughs again once or twice. I get up, enter the kitchen, fetch a silver glass, pour water, walk back, put it next to Dad, and sit back down. Dipping my fingers in the cold morning sand feels good. I lift some up and release it into the air. I watch the sand dance before resting on the ground. When Dad speaks again, he shifts my mind away from watching the sand falling from the palm of my hand.

"My brothers also died at a young age, and while my sister was watching the herds in the valley, she was abducted by the British army." The approach of death is jarring his soul and stirring up memories. His final agony is becoming a search for words, an effort to connect me to the bloodline, to the traditions of our family lineage. At the moment, however, I am only a preteen, forced to listen, unable to appreciate the significance of his words, unable to capture fully the finality of his life. It is his role to pass on these words of legacy, as it will be, one day, my role to do the same.

"Oh," I say. "I didn't know about any of that."

Lowering his gaze, Dad continues, "I did everything I could to prepare you for the harsh reality of this earth where only the strongest survives. I am an old man, and an old man often knows his time of death. My time of death is getting closer."

"I understand, Dad, yes, it's okay," I whisper in a sad voice. He puts his tongue over his lower lip and bites it softly while staring at the empty sky. He coughs and clears his throat and spits out gray mucus onto the sand.

"You are my son," Dad keeps repeating, as if to himself. He whispers in a low voice, rocking his head and letting me hear the rhythm of his words. I glance at his face. Illness is making him look eighty years old, but he is still in his forties. A red blanket is wrapped around his waist, and spikes of hair are poking out from his bare chest. His uncombed long, dark hair, gray on the sides, hangs over his dry face. Protruding veins cover his face. His eyes used to be as handsome as a baby's, but illness has created a playground of tiny red spots in the oval of his eyes like scattering ants. But the two deep dimples on his cheeks are still visible.

"Mmm," I murmur, not knowing how to reply. "Yes, Dad."

"You are my son," he repeats.

"Yes, Dad, you told me," I say in a suppressed voice.

"Uh-huh, I know," he wheezes. Dad coughs sporadically,

simultaneously clearing his throat. He looks woozy, and his mind is floundering. His eyes are fixed on me, and I remain as silent as the empty morning blue sky breaking into the light of midday.

"You will be the man in the house. Remember, you need to get an education, so you can help yourself and help others. I want you to protect the weak and to always be the giver. Be a good role model and help your mother."

Dad pushes his fingers into my Afro hair, and my glance switches between the sand and the pigeons waking up and flapping their wings for the first time today. Resting on top of their tiny birdhouse above the kitchen, the pigeons seem to stare at us.

"My time is nearing, and soon I shall not be here."

Dad rubs my head and wipes the tear hanging on my chin. He releases his cane and holds my hand. He kisses my hand and forehead. That kiss remains my only memory of affection between us. The tears standing in the oval of his eyes block him from saying more to me.

I rise and attempt to take a step away from him, but Dad still holds my hand. He walks, and I walk behind him. He enters his room and lies down on the floor mattress.

"Sit," he says. His words are making my eyes moist. Dad is in his early forties, his hair is mostly black, but he knows and I know and everyone else knows that he is dying. But death can't come until his veins refuse to carry blood through his body, until his heart suffocates and his breath ceases and his soul departs.

"I sent you to the valley to live with your grandmother when you were seven years old to teach you to live in a harsh landscape and prepare you for the reality of life."

"Mmm," I murmur. I look at him sitting in that room that smells of Vicks and vomit, with a portable IV line hanging from a pole next to the floor mattress.

"But I wish you had never sent me there," I suddenly blurt out.

"When I sent you to live in that valley with your grandmother, I never thought you would come back with polio," Dad confesses. "But this is your land, and regardless of how far you may drift away, this land is where you belong. You must learn to fight and defend what is yours."

"Mmm," I murmur. The Mogadishu July sun is now roasting everything below. I am rubbing a wet towel over his forehead.

"After you got polio, I knew you couldn't be a worker or a soldier like me, so I pushed you to go to school and become a professional. Remember, getting an education and finding a good job and helping others will benefit you in the end."

His head drops as if collapsing. Dad coughs and wheezes as his stomach gurgles. I turn and look at him while my fingers caress his bushy hair.

"Son, you carry my blood," he insists, rasping. His eyes are opening and closing as if he has lost control of them, but I still cannot imagine that his soul might soon drift away upward and over the clouds and the sky and pass through to the place where the dead find permanent residence. Still, as his soul is departing, I am forced to accept the idea that his lifeless body will soon decompose somewhere in the wilderness, somewhere in the soil, and ants will feed on it. I have a headache. I wish to see Dad in heaven chanting poetry and telling me to persevere in who I am and to know what I am.

"Son, you carry my blood," he growls, interrupting my

thoughts about death. "And the blood of all our departed souls."
I belong to a people of poetry, and there is poetry in saying
goodbye to souls departing and poetry in welcoming newborn
souls, poetry in declaring love and poetry in standing up to
the enemy.

However much Somalis may use words to appropriate meaning from struggle and death, we hesitate to express intimate
emotions in language. Some things are ineffable. We usually
do not utter the word *love*. I demonstrate my love for Dad by
sitting at his bedside, wiping his tears, cleaning the snot from
his cheeks, combing his hair, rubbing his back, giving him a
massage, and showing my teeth in a smile. And now, Dad, lying
on a floor mattress, is hovering between death and life. Heav-
ing and groaning, sobbing and coughing, he is desperately attempting to speak the very last chapter of his life.

When I find the strength to utter the word *love* to my dad,
I do not want anyone to hear me, although there is no one else
in the room. So I lower my head and draw my mouth close
to his ears and whisper, "I love you, Dad." He opens his eyes
slightly—or so I think—and I repeat "I love you" over and
over again. He opens his eyes, as if responding to the energy of
my love-confession, but continues to cough bitterly and heave.
Somewhere in the distance, I can hear Mama singing to herself
in a whispering voice as she hangs clothes up on the line. Why
is she singing? Doesn't she know what I am dealing with here?
Doesn't she understand that her husband is dying? Perhaps
she accepts the approach of Dad's demise. Perhaps she wants
to distract herself. Listening to her humming and clicking her
tongue, I just want to rush out of the room and clap my hands
and tap my feet and thus distract myself as well. Suddenly my
eyes rupture into tears. My heart hammers. My words morph

into hiccups and coughs. Dad's mouth hangs open. The angel of death is hovering.

"Mama," I call out.

Mama walks into the room and sees Dad struggling on his mat. He is still gasping for air, and his eyes have stopped blinking and remain open. She turns and leaves, only to come back a few minutes later with a man from the neighborhood.

"Surely we belong to Allah and to Him we shall return," the man says as he looks at Dad. Soon other men arrive to perform the ritual of Dad's dying. They stand in a circle around his mat and, with very little emotion, chant together in hushed tones, "Surely we belong to Allah and to Him we shall return."

While they stand over Dad's body, they are like stones, emotionless. As I attempt to chant with those seven poker-faced men, something in me does not like them. But I do not want my tears to betray me, so I lift up my sarong and wipe my eyes stealthily without them knowing it. Two men crouch down on either side of the mat as Dad lies between them. Still murmuring the death verses, one of them places his hand over Dad's eyes and mouth, and I hear him say, "Surely we belong to Allah and to Him we shall return. Death awaits us all."

"He's gone," one man says. "We shall all see him in the kingdom of death when our time comes."

No one cries. But the men sigh, clear their throats, and raise their heads to stare at the ceiling. At the moment when Dad is declared dead, I feel the air stop. The sun stops. My head spins. Everything around me seems to stop. A cold wind cut through my skin and crawls into my bones. My suppressed tears morph into hiccups. Thick, globular tears roll from my eyes. Life has lost its meaning. What am I going to do? Where am I going to go? What will my life be?

Word of Dad's death spreads like wildfire. A man wearing black-rimmed glasses walks into the room where Dad's body lies on that floor mattress. He is Dad's friend, and I often see him in the neighborhood, puffing on fat Cuban cigars. He always dresses in a black suit. As men gather around Dad's corpse, they fight back tears. Mama is crying behind the wall of her room, and all around me the wailing of women is rising and falling like the black pigeons in the neighborhood ascending and descending in the sky. The women's cries ricochet all around and into the neighborhood. Dad is gone, and he has left us—me; my twelve-year-old sister Hawo; my younger sisters, ten-year-old Murayo and five-year-old Taliso; my younger brothers, seven-year-old Bahdoon, three-year-old Hamud, and one-year-old Luqman. Our oldest sister had married and was living in the United States. My siblings, not understanding, are walking around as clueless as our goats. Death does not make sense.

The sun is tilting west, now turning yellow before it drops behind the horizon. In the bedroom, Dad's body is being washed. No longer in his own red blanket, he is wrapped in a white cloth like a mummy. The casket stands next to Dad's body, ready to take him away forever. My stomach softens with the thought that the casket might protect Dad from decay and from ants eating him. A commotion of men murmuring "God is great" fills the air, and not far behind trails the wail of women, repeating words in confused rhythms. Men walk out carrying Dad's casket. Outside, a horde of men swarms around the casket. As they emerge from the room, men rush to their Jeeps, Toyotas, Fiats, Alfa Romeo sedans, VW beetles, GMCs, and other vehicles, opening the doors, climbing in, and taking their seats. Diverse engines roar all at once. The men load the coffin onto the open bed of a light-duty blue mini truck. Many men climb up and stand in a circle over Dad's coffin. They cast their eyes down, pinch their lips, and murmur something. The truck moves like a turtle, and other vehicles reverse and line up as far as my eyes can see. All I can think of is how horrible it will feel to leave Dad in a forest grave, and I intend to return whenever I can to whisper prayers over his grave.

The funeral cortege turns right into the forest cemetery and stops. The sand is soft and red. The trees are thicker, spread flat and horizontally, but some trees swirl, and the birds on the branches chirp. The men getting down from their vehicles remind me of monkeys climbing down from trees. The Quran teacher has chosen a gravesite for Dad between two large trees with connecting upper branches. It is the perfect place for him to rest. I promise him I will return and visit.

The Quran teacher grabs a shovel and begins to dig, and the rest of the men follow suit in silence. Dad is lowered into the grave, his head facing east, and laid to rest.

As mourners return to our house, a feast of rice, meat, and tea awaits them. A cup of tea is handed around and makes its way to me, but I pass it on to the old man with combed hair sitting next to me.

"No, you drink it yourself," he says, looking at me from beneath his bushy gray eyebrows, hair tufting from his nose and ears.

Dad taught me to yield my place, my tea, and my food to elders and to allow them to speak first, even if they are stupid.

"No, I insist," I reply.

"I shall not drink before the agoon," the man replies, using the Somali word for orphan. *Agoon* for a Somali is more than an orphan. An *agoon* is isolated from society, meaningless, used, discarded. Since my father has died, this elder is labeling me an outcast, an object of pity and scorn. How dare he call me *agoon*!

"I am not an orphan," I declare in a hesitant, low voice. As soon as I speak, heads turn and eyes stare, as if I am saying something wrong.

"What?" The elder grunts as he wraps his long red-and-white scarf around his shoulders and adjusts the cap on his head. Those garments symbolized wisdom gained with the passing of time, and most male elders in the neighborhood wear similar caps.

"Nothing," I say. "Never mind."

"Okay. Drink your tea," he insists.

Two sips into the hot tea, I feel the stomach cramps worsen until I get up and walk away from that old man with the teacup in my hand. I drop the cup, and then watch the tea stain the sand.

"I am not an orphan," I say to myself. I turn away from his face to stare at the neighborhood monkey sitting in a neighboring tree. The monkey belongs to no one—no one wants him. Or perhaps he too is *agoon*. When God yanks my father's soul and takes it away, does he really make me *agoon*? When armed men chase me away from my valley, do they really make me *agoon*? When white American cops and all my American co-workers refuse me a livelihood, do they really make me *agoon*? And isn't the black man in America something of an *agoon*? When your country rejects you, where do you belong? You are really nothing, but *agoon* like me. I have become part of that black experience, and we are *agoon* in this land of original sin. Now, more than forty years old, I remain nothing but *agoon*, on the move and still running.

Sitting in the airplane cabin, Mama is looking at the TV.

When I hear her cough, I begin to worry a bit. As I look over at her, she returns my look with a smile of her own, as if she is telling me, *Don't worry. I don't have COVID.*

I notice a man who resembles my father, dead now for more than thirty years. The man looks just like my father. His scruffy beard. His deep dimples. His bushy eyelashes. His light skin. His dark lips. He looks just like my father.

My eyes close, and I doze off.

My father visits me. He is wearing white.

Looking at him, I see his hair is shaved on the sides, but he has dreadlocks and a braided ponytail. I like the freedom of his hair. His face is clear of the pimples I remember.

Oh, his bushy eyebrows, which I also remember, are trimmed to perfection like the green grass of America. But above all, I like the freedom of his hair. His eyes are as clear as a baby's. He extends his hand to reach mine, but I hesitate.

"My son," he says.

"Is it really you? My father!"

"My son. How I have missed you."

Tears gush from my eyes and roll down my chin. My armpits itch.

It is strange to see my father walking on snow as if he is familiar with the experience.

When he sits down on a rock covered with snow, I am very conscious of the fact that he does not belong to the snow. Maybe he is here to protect me from the sharp sting of that falling snow.

"Come to me, my son."

A single white sarong is wrapped around his waist, and another hangs from his upper body. But I am thinking that my father must be freezing. I want to tell him to wear a jacket, but my words seem to choke in me. I can only cry, not speak to him.

I sit next to him. Each time I want to touch his hand, I cannot.

I feel a weight pressing on my hand.

"Father," I yell out, but he has trouble hearing me.

"My son. My brave son, we haven't sat together for a long time."

Then my father begins to chant a poem, as we did once or twice before in Mogadishu, sitting beneath a flock of pigeons flying high and then low against the silhouette of that sun with its yellow, orange, and red variations. Before I know it, the movement of our lips are one.

Our humming merges and lifts and flies away like those birds.

Be the knower of words
Be the brave
Know the enemy
Know your history
Know your birth

Just know
I am the settler
Of the bright cave
I am the knower
I am your father

You are not
The black
Or the white

And the yellow
You are the sun

Be you
You are the knower
Of the snow
A waiter of death
You are a traveler
The fearer of history
The defender of my legacy
The bearer of my blood
You are my son

As I extend my hand to touch his, my father vanishes. Gone. My body remains in the seat. I open my eyes, and tears well up. And I see Mama sitting next to me, awake.

"Mama," I say. "How are you feeling?"

"Fine," she replies.

The plane is descending through the air toward land. America is behind us. Africa is drawing nearer. My nostrils are picking up the memory scent of that Nugaal Valley.

Looking out, I see a rainbow.

The sky is a bit gray, as if rain is coming.

ACKNOWLEDGMENTS

HER LOVE. HER TEARS. HER PAIN. HER HUNGER. A FALLEN STAR, still standing. The drifting wind, still in the air. To my mother, Halimo, who went through catastrophe to get me out of the African wars and to help me get through America's wars against black bodies. To the mothers at war. Mothers raising children in the ghetto. Mothers in Ukraine. Mothers in Afghanistan. Syrian mothers. I dedicate this book not only to my dear mother, the star of my world, but to all mothers around the world.

I am a man with distinctly different cultures in two different countries. In the culture of Ayeyo, my grandmother, we honor those whom we adore with camels. One camel is for my adopted America and its complex generosity. And the other two camels are for Alicia Brooks, my wonderful literary agent at the Jean Naggar Literary Agency, and for Amber Oliver, an editor at Penguin Random House, who first believed in my written words. A camel for Noah Eaker, my awesome editor at Harper, and another camel for John Ralston Haynes, a friend, a mentor, and an editor. For you all, here I am standing on the white sand beach city of Eyl, Somalia, taking my hat off and glancing at the falling yellow sun. I am drinking camel's milk in your honor.

ABOUT THE AUTHOR

BOYAH J. FARAH's writing has been featured in the *Guardian*, the *Harvard Transition*, *Grub Daily*, and *Truthdig*, and on the *Scheer Intelligence* podcast at KCRW. He is the winner of *Salon*'s best essay of 2017. His essays have also appeared in Harvard's *Kennedy School Review*, *Pangyrus* magazine, and the *Huffington Post*. He recently founded the Abaadi Center in Garowe, Somalia, which offers instruction in English, Math, and Science to students age thirteen to twenty-four.